PALESTINE INCIDENTALLY

Cliff G Hanley

ISBN 13: 9781484066546

For Jo

Also by Cliff G Hanley

The Red Guitar
Springheeled Kate
Not Being Dead and other tales

PALESTINE INCIDENTALLY

Taking a journey, for whatever reason, is an opportunity to live your life in microcosm. You can, if you are able, try out versions of yourself before resurfacing, and if you have lived long enough, perform running repairs on your personality and psyche. Any community travelling together with a common purpose has to learn quickly how to love and tolerate – it's a basic survival technique. On the road, everyone's strengths and weaknesses become exaggerated, which should, in theory at least, make this easier.

Even writing about this is a kind of journey, and I hope that my friends will extend their tolerance this much further.

Concerned only with making my mark as a musician, I paid little attention to foreign affairs in the 1980s, although I befriended the writer and entrepreneur Bill Hopkins, who I found by accident: I was moving from flat to flat and had no settled address in London, and he owned an antique shop full of antiques which he only rarely could be persuaded to sell; The Postcard Shop, in Kensington Park Road, with a notice in the window advertising as a mailing address. Just what I needed; and in the days before mobile phones and email, the best you could get, if trying to do business with no fixed abode. Bill edited and wrote a lot of the contents of the news magazine, Arab World, which was deliberately made to resemble Time Magazine; being a designer myself, I noticed its appearance first - and I had some part to play in that as I became employed to illustrate the covers for a few years, plus the occasional heading. That association came to an end when the magazine's backer died and his widow (and heir) left the country. At the same time, Israel had mounted an advertising exercise to get British holidaymakers to try the sun in Eliat or the Dead Sea. There were big posters all over London Tube. As I was becoming vaguely aware from headlines that somewhere up in the hills above Israel was Palestine, and that there was some kind of disagreement in the air that went beyond rivalry, I started to think that it would be more interesting and also more balanced to go the hills instead, despite the Palestinians being unable to speak for themselves so effectively through either advertising or the news media - or perhaps in fact because of that.

My holiday plans were put on hold until I found myself, through a series of accidents, living in the West Country town of Bristol, where I found it only too easy to immerse myself in the political activity bubbling under all round me. Sue, a member of the local Palestine Solidarity Campaign, had been visiting that country at least once a year for around a decade, and knew all about how to get there; her most recent visit to Bethlehem coincided with the military incursion and so much of her stay was under curfew, and the experience must have been less than lively. After hearing her talk about this visit, her twentieth, I begged her to take me along next time. She called me on the 6th August 2002 to confirm the trip. About half a dozen were going together by plane in November, hoping for a good look at Palestine.

It seemed to me that for Bristolians, or at least those in the broadest circle I drifted into, a visit to Palestine had become 'what one does'. The level of left-wing political activity was pretty high in Bristol, with the Stop The War group and the long-running peace vigil, the Palestine Solidarity Campaign branch, support for parties like Socialist Alliance and, later, Respect, and support campaigns for immigrants. You might hear Palestine spoken of in the same casual terms as once you may have heard about Blackpool, Rhyl or Rothesay; more recently Ibiza or Mallorca.

The first time I would get to speak to a real, Israeli-in-

the-street guy was when we shared seats on the return plane. We got on fairly well skirting round the big issue and getting into movies, which is one of my two dead-cert topics. We had one thing in common - a temporary memory lapse about the name Almodovar. Then, as the much-delayed plane soared over the night-lights of Tel Aviv/Jaffa, he gestured at the window, intoning in pride and wonder, 'Just look at that - and to think that only fifty years ago it was all sand and rock.'
'Hmm,' I replied, our nascent friendship taking a hard knock from my lack of evident enthusiasm.

As we flew in, the first we had seen of Palestine was Tel Aviv, which in the hard blast of the November sun looked to me a little like a high-density Easterhouse. The business of entering the country took an interminable time, including the temporary loss of our passports and an interrogation for Sue. This was an illuminating experience; probably no worse than trying to enter the UK as an alien with the wrong kind of skin.

The journey to Bethlehem was pretty straightforward for this country: no changing of transport, only one roadblock, outside Jerusalem, and we were allowed to stay in the mini-bus while our passports were scrutinised. There were eight of us with the 140-bed Star Hotel to ourselves. I was sharing with John, a retired doctor. The next day he negotiated a room of his own, which seemed fair given the vacancy situation. It occurred to me on the third day though, as John had been hit with an attack of the 'runs' while my own digestive system seized up, if we had continued to share, perhaps our respective sheng fuis might have established an equilibrium.

Sue introduced us to the hotel manager, Achmed. On this our first night, his brother Ahmed and sister-in-law Rima visited with their baby. All the girls had to have a 'shot'. We learned that although Ahmed studied political economy in Syria, he had to seek work as a cop.

Our first full day, Saturday, began with John and me breaking Sue's number one rule by each exploring the local streets, before being shown round by the expert; the combination of the beautiful weather and early morning bustle being irresistible. After breakfast everyone piled off into a little bus for the day's treat - a visit to Deisheh Refugee Camp, with one of Sue's many good friends here: Jusef, a camp resident. Repeated references to such places in the UK news media as 'camps' have fixed the wrong impression in the public eye Although many would have started as tent cities for people who believed they would be able to return to their homes in a few days, they are well-established built communities; fifty-nine of which are in neighbouring countries but many in Palestine itself, for internal exiles.

At the camp's entry road stood a monument of sorts, commemorating the time before the Palestinian Authority took over administering the camp. A ten-foot-high turnstile.

Our first stop here was at the medical centre; run, as was the whole camp, by UNWRA (UN relief and Works agency for Palestine and the Near East). A staff nurse mentioned her day-today problems: getting drugs from Jerusalem especially when there are major clampdowns on movement; the most prevalent illnesses among Palestinians being bronchitis, flu and stress-related problems, the last affecting teenagers in particular. The camp manager Hussein Shahim took the time to greet us, and to give us a short talk, starting with1948/49, when one million Jews immigrated to Palestine and thousands of Palestinians were made homeless. Refugees can be found all over the country and not only in 'camps'. In 1950, he continued, most of the homeless fled east to the Jordan River and a UNWRA was set up to deal with what was generally seen as a temporary problem. The 1967 war increased the problems for refugee camps with Israeli occupation. The effect of the Gulf War on Deisheh Camp was to make it a virtual prison. Thousands were arrested, many were locked up and possibly 'disappeared'.

By 1993 the camp was a military zone. No-one was able to work without a permit from the Israeli aithorities; this led to an unemployment level of 85%. The camp was restricted in size to 360 *durhams*. For the increasing population the only option was, and remains, to build upwards. The next landmark was the Oslo Negotiations, which although they were mostly in Israel's favour, recognised the need for some kind of justice and a partial right of return. They were ignored by Israel.

Since the beginning of the Second Intifada, life has been much more difficult. All cities and villages have been isolated, with roadblocks at the few exits left open and ID cards being compulsory. In the camp, food rations were distributed every four months by UNWRA, which also provided schooling and an admin office which has the discretion to provide more help for 'special cases'.

Deisheh Camp grew up on the road between Jerusalem and south Bethlehem. Like all the camps it began as a literal row of tents; it grew to hold 2,300 families from Jerusalem and 46 nearby villages, most of which have been razed.

We thanked Hussein for starting the process of opening our eyes, and Jusef took us off to his home. On his roof we had a fine view of the forests of water tanks clustered on all Palestinian rooftops, vital additions as the army regularly destroys water conduits and much of the country's supplies are diverted to the 'settlements' (Jewish colonies) which are also not rows of tents.)Fortress citadel is an appropriate description although some resemble British council housing estates. The water tanks are among the first casualties of joyshooting soldiers whoever there are incursions. Up here we could also spot a few rubble-strewn lots where the army bulldozers had executed biblical justice on resistance suspects and their relatives, as well as the other two rooftop self-sufficiences: solar panels and chickens. We were all handed little cups of strong, sweet coffee, (a note for gourmands here: the lady of the house was glad to share her secret with me: some cardamom was ground in with the coffee), and soon we were ushered back down inside for a wonderful meal of chicken and vegetables in wraps. Our host, having allowed us good time for the meal to sink in, now took us out again to the densely built-up community to visit two brothers: the house their families shared was the first stop last time the army invaded. All occupants, they told us, were herded into one room and had to stay there with no access to food, water or plumbing while the soldiers 'looking for terrorists', took their home apart: slashing furniture, knocking a hole in the wall and emptying all jars of grain, rice and lentils into one heap topped by the stock of olive oil, all stirred well as they shouted, 'We're cooking something nice for you!'

After the families were let out, all males were tied up, blindfolded and taken away to a local school for some 'interrogation.' We had all read about this kind of stuff, but it was quite visceral hearing it directly from the victims in their partially repaired homes.

A few weeks before our visit, one of my paintings was auctioned for Palestine. I was carrying most of the money and could feel it threatening to burst into flames in my pocket. I was only too glad of the chance to unload some of it, so Jusef got some to divvy out to his neighbours. Later in the week I could give him a share for himself. One of the ways in which he fed his beautiful family was by exporting olive-wood carvings - his next trip, planned for December, was postponed by yet another Israeli clampdown.

November in Palestine: although it was strictly mad dog weather in blazing contrast to the grudging trickle of British summer, we schlepped onwards. At the top of the hill overlooking Deisheh we met a grizzly-bearded guy who greeted us with a warm and hearty cry of 'Balfour Declaration!'
Above his house was a partly-built hotel - work abandoned for the present - and two well-aged ambulances, the windscreen of one peppered with bullet holes from only a few months back.

In the evening, Sue arranged a visit to the hotel by the

Deputy Education Officer for Bethlehem accompanied by Jack, one of the three brothers who own the hotel. They were unable to demonstrate any shred of hope for the future; their only wishes were for their children as their own lives had been destroyed. Children are traumatised from birth, and their education is subject to constant interruption, which in turn affects their ability to cope with university if they get that far. They have no future; not the kind of well-fed 'no future' that Johnny Rotten was yelling about in the 'seventies, but in a literal sense: the only industry open to them, tourism, devastated by the wide-spread belief that this is a permanent war-zone. There was little chance of persuading these kids to stop looking to suicide bombers as glamorous, heroic figures. We were advised, 'Forget about going on protest marches. If only makes you feel better. Better to refuse to pay your taxes, or tell your churches to complain about the persecution of their people, and the denial of access to holy places.'

I had to agree, as a Ban the Bomb veteran going back to 1959.

On Sunday we took advantage of that rare access, and the Godfearing, or merely curious members of our party visited church, while we aetheists bought some beads and hats in Manger Square, impersonating the huge droves of tourists who previously swarmed through the town. The Star is only one of several large hotels in Bethlehem, all practically empty. Later we all strolled up Milk Grotto Street, stepping over a row of stumps where the tanks had been inconvenienced by trees and streetlights. In the Milk Chapel we met Father Lawrence, who gave us a sales-pitch about the Grotto's efficacy in boosting the fertility of childless couples. One side chapel was lined with dated photos of satisfied pairs; I could see though, that people have gone over to science since the First Intifada. Another sign of the time of the tanks was the rows of bites taken out of nearly every pavement kerb, as tanks are blind in confined spaces and have to navigate by grinding and bumping. That also explains the fact that on houses and walls all electrical conduits and exterior drainpipes were brand new. The little park surrounding us was the only place of its kind in Bethlehem, Father Lawrence pointed out, adding that the Order had plans for another chapel on that site. For the citizens of Bethlehem who like to loll about on the grass, the only alternative is their surrounding hills, which are forbidden territory. The town, charming and bucolic as it might appear to visitors, is in effect, like all non-Zionist, non-Jewish Palestinian towns and surviving villages, effectively a jail. There was no question of expansion and as with the camps, peripheral building has to be upwards.

John, Pauline Eileen and I found out more about this territorial business when we accidentally came across the university - which at least one of us didn't expect to find in this isolated little town. We timed it well: it was graduation day. Three months late, as the original date inconveniently coincided with the campus being requisitioned by the Israeli army. We found the Academic Vice-Chancellor, a Christian Brother from America. He explained that the university was built with funds from Switzerland, Holland and Canada, plus regular support from the Vatican. He directed our gaze to the two local 'settlements' - Har Homa and Gilo, and the unmistakeable bridge which links the second of these to yet another colony, via a tunnel under the hill town of Beit Jala. Thus Israelis may travel without the unsettling experience of touching Palestine. A new road was growing round the base of the hills these fortresses covered. Outside the road there was a broad no-go strip and fence. The plan, no secret, was to eventually have Bethlehem completely ringed off.

During the previous incursion. Brother Neil and his colleagues were confined to the premises for forty days, as was all of town to its homes. The campus, ostensibly an elegant, restful and modern/classical establishment including an ampitheatre taking advantage of the hill's natural slope has details not found in most universities: bullet holes, mostly on the Har Homa side, and a sizable shell-hole in the library wall. The soldiers, after firing on the campus, searched and then occupied it, claiming that snipers were based there.

We left the newly gowned graduates to their shady cloisters and strolled off downhill past a clutch of quite grand houses (built for wealthy Christians who, as we later heard, had since left Palestine), and Beit Jala refugee camp, which is joined at the elbow to Bethlehem. A café appeared up the back side of the hill, and we gently stampeded towards it. Although it had practically nothing for sale except tea and fizzy drinks, we collapsed gratefully in its shade and enjoyed the vibes. It's *the* place to hang around if you're a teenager, I could see. Not far along was another café though, with… ice cream. The Arab nations, who invented sweets, continue to produce the world's finest ice cream; in a class, really, of its own. Thus fortified, we soon returned up-town by a back road we missed before. There was a little shop selling washing powder, mops and clothes-pegs, run by a respectable gent in a sharp suit. He was a parks manager before the Intifada. His friend, a guy from Jordan, told me he was less mobile than he would prefer since a roadblock soldier took his passport and scissored it into pieces. 'Why?' I asked. 'I asked him why. He said - because he felt like it!'

After nightfall, Tony and Colin, two computer wizards in the outside world, yielded to the need for some old-fashioned mindlessness and jumped in a taxi for The Tent, a local eatery, for a proper drink and a hookah experience. By Monday it was time for everyone to do the Big City, which meant getting a taxi to the roadblock, queuing with passports and getting a bus on the other side. This is daily reality for those Palestinians who have managed to obtain travel permits. It can be such a time-waster that many workers and students, I was told, just leave home permanently to be where they want (and need) to work.

Our exploration of the ancient city of Jerusalem began at the Jaffa Gate We plunged into the crowded maze, some parts more tunnels than lanes and found our way to the Church of the Holy Sepulchre, a venerable palimpsest of architecture and cultures - the common source of all the Judeo/Islam/Christian religions was manifest in its walls. In the interior you will find several 'strip cartoons' made of paint or mosaic, all depicting the last days of Jesus, dating from Byzantium to a few years ago. In the immediate surroundings we enjoyed relative quiet, joined only by a man and his donkey, plus several passing soldiers and armed police, as we stopped for an al fresco caffeine boost. Sue took us next to Ali Jaber's antique shop. Another of Sue's good friends, Ali summed up the situation in Palestine, saying things would get worse before they get better. His wife couldn't help run the shop because she wasn't allowed a travel permit. 'She couldn't share things like looking after the children, picking them up after school. 'One day,' he said, 'a soldier took my permit and peeled the backing off, just like that. I can still use it, but I must replace it soon. To do that I have to wait in a queue, for as long as a week. I asked him, 'Why did you do that?' He said 'don't you dare tell me I did that!' I said it again. I shouted. He brings other soldiers out. They threatened me if I didn't shut up. But I refused!' He touched on life in the camp, illuminated by his sardonic sense of humour. It's between Jerusalem, closed to all without travel permits, and Ramallah, curfewed off at six p.m., 'So you are advised not to get seriously ill at night.' He spoke, too, of America, of US citizens living in a 'golden room', a room without windows. After saying goodbye to Ali. We passed near the Wailing Wall, which involved going through an airport-style security gate mid-souk. Near the Wall I noticed two distinct groups of people: young girls with big guns and orthodox Jews. I asked one of the second group, an American, where I could get a decent hat. Sue pointed out the tunnel leading from the square to the Aqsa Mosque, used by Arial Sharon's route when his visit set off the Second Intifada. We didn't even consider visiting a mosque; since a hard-line Zionist tried blowing one up, round here they are strictly for Muslims only. And wailing was also not on the agenda - we followed our noses to a hole-in-the-wall café for a sublime, huge meal of falafel and salad.

In the evening we were invited to Rima and Mohammed's for talk, fruit and yet more wonderful Arabic coffee. Rima couldn't understand my fractured Moroccan-Arabic and maybe thought I was pulling her leg, so we all stuck to English.
Tuesday's adventure was a visit to Ramallah, so it was out with the passports again. A taxi to the roadblock, bus to the Damascus Gate, Jerusalem, where Sue found a minibus driven by an 'Israeli' Palestinian, Issa, who took us through a roadblock on the edge of Jerusalem, then another, very crowded and very busy one, at Ramallah. Our driver became our guide and companion on the journey . His well-known face plus Sue's soft talk got us through with considerable ease, past most of the queue and with our only having to show our passports from the comfort of our seats this of course added to our sense of guilt.. At one of these checkpoints, we later learned, a Palestinian was being beaten up away from our foreigners' prying eyes.

Before hitting the dirty city proper, we stopped off at what remained of Yasser Arafat's compound. Only two buildings were standing; one appeared to have had a recent facelift and rebuilding continued. Amongst enormous heaps of rubble not merely blown up, but flattened out by giant army bulldozers, themselves as big as houses. There was also what appeared to be the parking-lot, a huge mound of burnt-out, mashed up cars and other unidentifiable vehicles. In the UK you would not be allowed anywhere near a site like this without a helmet. Here, two venerable gentlemen sat comfortably in their rescued stacking chairs, watching the building work, and the abrupt appearance of TV and radio crews thrusting a forest of mics at Saeb Erekat, the Palestinian Negotiator. Above them hung huge chunks of broken concrete, dangling on wires. They don't care! Like those who live their lives in the shadow of the volcano...

In Ramallah proper, Eileen managed to direct us to the Tamer Institute. Here, two ladies found the time to welcome us - the Director Jehan Helou and her assistant, from Nablus, who mentioned in her preamble that her husband is from Haifa; neither of them, having left home, could get back to visit their respective families. It can be like that: once out, always out. Jehan told us about the work of the Institute: They encourage children to write, local and outside writers to contribute work, and publish it all, well illustrated and distributed to 64 libraries throughout Palestine. One recent project was to get children conducting interviews with their local elders, to construct oral histories. This was not as simple as it sounds, given the restrictions on travel. Overall, the point of the Institute through these domestic projects and overseas schemes is to give the children of Palestine something hopeful and creative to focus on.

Our interview was interrupted twice: first by an explosion outside and the howls of emergency vehicles. Jehan smiled indulgently at our alarm, telling us they are used to this, only listening to where the ambulances or fire engines may be headed, to guess the location. The second interruption was for hospitality. Heaps of bread, soaking in oil and sprinkled with zataar (that peculiarly Palestinian blend of herbs including thyme) and cheese, and washed down with mint and sage tea. Colin marvelled at how much of this stuff I could put away. I admitted that food is my favourite drug; and this combination of simplicity and subtlety was irresistible.

We all took our leave and let our hosts get back to work, splitting up for a short exploration of the city centre. It was raining, but Ramallah, with its colourful confusion of crowds, garish shop signs and freely improvised traffic was very much like downtown Bombay - or Saigon. We plunged in regardless. Sue warned us though, that if we stayed too long we might be caught up in the evening curfew. The road home took us through another roadblock where our guide made as much as he could of his cargo of foreigners, getting us past the huddled masses and lines of traffic, saving us from what looked like a three-hour wait. Instead of heading straight on here we had to detour via a new freeway built to service one of the ubiquitous 'settlements', where we paused for a quick photo shoot. The next glitch was one of the temporary 'pop-up' checkpoints that spring up anywhere, at any time, for no apparent reason other than to make life difficult. And a taxi to the hotel. I could see how this routine would lose its novelty value.

In the evening we were treated to a visit from the Minister for Tourism, Kamal el Qaisi. Obviously he wasn't at his busiest, although he was about to take off for a short promotional tour of Europe. He agreed with the advice Sue gave me: we should send all notes, names and addresses to ourselves in envelopes rather than risk losing them to the customs people at the airport. And to send them from Jerusalem, as the post service in the West Bank is very slow and unreliable. He had his own perspective on life in Palestine. Although he had joint Italian/Palestinian citizenship, as far as the Israeli

Government was concerned he was 'just another Palestinian'. He couldn't fly out from Tel Aviv, but had to leave the country by the Jordan Bridge. There was no point, he said, in booking a plane in advance, as he had no guarantee of even getting to Amman and certainly none for the length of his journey there. Of one thing he was certain: the constant humiliation of dealing with Israel's boy soldiers, who have no respect for age or position. 'If an Israeli soldier cannot kill you with bullets, he kills you with words.'

He gave us a brief resumé of the April invasion. Two or three thousand soldiers and 250 tanks crowded into the narrow lanes and streets of Bethlehem to subdue a population of 24,000. For 17 days the curfew was total. No doors, no windows could be opened, on pain of death. After five days, Kamal el-Qaisi phoned the Italian Embassy for help, as his son needed milk. The consul-General arranged for a delivery by Italian journalists but when Kamal tried to take the milk from them, the soldiers ordered him to turn back or be shot. Eventually the Red Cross got through and Kamal was able to share some milk with his neighbours. One of the brave locals who tried to get food to those trapped in the Church was shot, and as no one was allowed to help him, he lay in the Square until he died. After 17 days people were allowed out of their homes for two hours, to do some shopping, but as there probably wasn't much stock left in the shops apart from jeans, bicycle inner tubes, clothes-pegs, there would not have been much of nutritional value. Before that 'break' one old lady and her son had visitors: some soldiers decided against knocking on the door and just flattened the house.

'The Israelis,' said Kamal, 'will use the war with Iraq to expel as many Palestinians into Jordan as possible. For those who remain, life will be more and more difficult; punishment and restrictions - the hope that they, too, will leave.'

Kamal, although he could take his family off into Italy, feels that he is a Palestinian above all, and could never think of being anywhere else.. As Eileen observed, this seemed typical of the mixture of pessimism and resolve we found everywhere.

The 'boys' almost persuaded me to join them for another wild night at The Tent, but I decided to have a look at Bethlehem by night. It's almost inexpressively beautiful, the sparse lighting giving the lanes, passages and houses completely new dimensions; chiaroscuro suddenly bursting into vignets of ancient stone and cobbles. The cats rule the streets now - as they are all round the Mediterranean all Palestinian cats are feral and their world, although concurrent with ours, is completely separate. It's a jungle down there. When the day's market trading is done they perform some of the function of the free-ranging cows of India, hoovering up much of the waste. Don't expect them to show any gratitude though. They have good reason to distrust humans, particularly in Bethlehem, where so many of them were killed walking into the auto-sniper's lazer-beam trained on the entrance to the Church of the Nativity.

On my return I found Pauline chatting to Achmed, hotel manager. Over a coke or two, we talked for a while. Achmed strayed into the subject of his having trouble with balance, which he suspected may have been caused by the dark 17 days. The hotel was turned into an army barracks (after Jack pleaded with the Israelis not to destroy it as they had already done with his other hotel - If they did, there would be nothing left for his family, who would, he confided, be as well becoming bombers), and for all that time Achmed had no sleep, running and fetching for the soldiers; '-or it might have been the time I was in jail.'

How could that affect balance? I immediately thought of the Guildford Four in England, but this went beyond 'mere' beating and sleep deprivation. For Achmed jail meant fifteen days and nights half-standing, hands tied, in a cell no bigger than a coffin. He had also experienced the dreadful and infamous 'chair' torture. I sat there, looking at this ordinary guy, someone like you and me, talking in this comfortable lounge about these outlandish experiences in such a matter-of-fact way - and felt my hold on reality slipping away.

Next morning, we visited the building where the cat sniper was placed: The Peace Center. Say what you want about the Zionist regime, but you could never accuse it of being without a sense of irony. The Peace Center was a shiny modern arts conglomerate, with a bookshop, a tourist info centre, conference facilities and three galleries. The director, Michel Nasser, inevitably had evidence of less balmy days. During the insurgency the building was occupied for 38 days during which the soldiers stole a recently excavated Byzantine mosaic and trashed just about everything else - furniture, doors, toilets, computers. The electricity was de-earthed, leaving every part of the building a danger to life. The main entrance was left untouched for the benefit of the world's TV cameras. When Sweden, perhaps Palestine's chief benefactor, complained about the damage, Israeli

Government replied that 'only' 1,000 shekels-worth of damage had been done, and that the rest would *of course* have been done by Palestinian vandals after the army left. It was time for us to wave Pauline off, as she was leaving a couple of days before the end of the week. The afternoon was cool enough for Janet, Eileen and I to risk a walk up to the village of Beit Jala. Halfway up the other side of the valley, the girls spotted a shop front bearing the sign, 'Lifegate Center'. Nosey as always, we sneaked inside to look for signs of life. The director of the Center, a German, welcomed us in and we chatted for a while. It turned out that this is a charity for disabled youngsters, supported by German churches. If there's anywhere that Europe can be said to gel into a single purposeful entity, it must be Palestine. Many of the disabilities here are the result of village inbreeding, marriage between cousins being common. Disability tended to be seen as ' the will of Allah', but there was a weekly club for mothers, where some kind of genetic counselling took place. I couldn't begin to imagine what form that would take, or what it would achieve; but the major work was hands-on and practical. There were four flats where young people could learn to look after themselves. The Director handed us over to Susie, a blonde ex-copper from Fulham, London, and married to a Palestinian. Susie gave us a quick tour of the workshops - woodwork, embroidery, knitting, blacksmithing and finally the olive pickling room, overseen by a girl who, I thought, was a recognisable Palestine 'type' - long legs, sharp cheekbones. As we turned finally to left, she rewarded me with a look of surprise when I said, 'Ma'asalemah.'

We also got to hear about the Arab Rehabilitation Centre, which has gradually become a hospital dealing with bomb, bullet and landmine injuries. In the village we could see where many of these injuries would originate - the side hanging over the bridge and facing the settlement looked a little like a mouthful of smashed teeth. Several houses were being rebuilt, I was told, with funds from two or three European countries. Beit Jala was an intricate tumble of ancient homes, steep lanes and churches. Most of its inhabitants were professed Christians, and most of them appeared to be children, whose numbers were almost equalled by the cats, a large family of which had taken over a skip. We wandered, gobsmacked, through this community of gardens and balconies, helped on our way by the cool, fragrant breeze and the birdlike babble of the kids practising their bits of English. In the square we got talking to one parent, who took us up to the side of the village immediately close to the bridge. From here, looking down, we could see that the bridge was completely enclosed. Our guide handed us over to his friend, who showed us the Greek Orthodox church, where there was a small crowd of men, fresh from the funeral of one of the Fathers. The church had just been fitted with new bells at the expense of the Russian Orthodox Church. The old bells, as old as the village itself, and we knew that that must be very old indeed, were propped up on the ground. They were brought down by Israeli shells (or perhaps a sniper). Eileen wondered if this was the next best thing to destroying the church itself, which might have been bad PR. One guy I spoke to, perhaps in his seventies, gestured behind him at the settlement on the hill. 'That was my farm!'

As we left, we wished our new friends good luck.

'We do not need good luck. We trust in the grace of

God,' came the reply, demonstrating that faith can transcend experience. Janet looked back at this prettiest of villages and exclaimed, 'I'd love to die here!'
I, ever the old cynic, replied, 'It could probably be arranged.'
On our way back we hit the wrong road, and thus serendipitously meant asking the way from Johnny, a guy who runs a local TV station. His 'thing' is old movies, so old movies jostled with phone-ins for space in the broadcasts, while daytime TV comprised mainly a digest of Israeli news. One 'ahah!' thing he mentioned was: most Israelis don't know what is happening here; just like the Sun readers in the UK, they probably only get a heavily biased breakdown of 'hot' news, leavened with opinion and rumour. The daily grind of humiliation and death that is Palestinian living will be unknown, and the only time they are liable to be aware of Palestinians will be when one of them inexplicably blows up.

Next day we headed for Jerusalem again. The first of the roadblocks had a tank standing by; we heared this was because it was the start of Ramadan, which increases state paranoia just as the Ghost Dance worried the European invaders in America a hundred and something years back. There is no avoiding the US connection on any level - the gun culture has been exported to Palestine. You may grow up in a society where it's acceptable for Daddy to sleep with a .38 under his pillow. The more guns your home contains, the more threatened you feel, although the weapons are intended to bring security. This is repeated on a national level - the USA, the most impregnable and heavily armed country in the world, is obsessed with threats from '*out there*'. We can see this pattern of thought taking hold in the UK too: now that British policemen are being armed as a matter of course, they appear to be more afraid of potential gun attacks than before. If you come from a country where it is your 'right' to own the means for killing those with whom you disagree, and take your family to the Promised Land, heavily subsidised by the Israeli Government (which in the end would mean US taxpayers), you will naturally feel free to shoot and shell the 'others', particularly when your new home is built on what was their land, and you have heard that they may try to get it back.

There are, though, many shades of opinion in Israel. We visited a suburb resembling Los Angeles: big trees, beautiful gardens and security cameras everywhere. 'Peace Now' has its offices here, and we were lined up for a talk with Reuven Kaminer, who wised us up to the good news. Peace Now exists mainly to help the young people who refuse conscription to oppress Palestine, and to provide support for their families. The growing levels of refusniks led the government to bring in mercenaries including the Druze Militia, who tended to be particularly unbiased in their ruthlessness. The refusniks, about 65% of those called up, either used 'influence' or volunteered for alternative work, or otherwise were going to jail. This might have been only for a few months at most, according to Reuven, they are not treated badly and rearrests are infrequent. 'They are Israeli citizens, after all, and have rights.' But I wouldn't deny their bravery. And the alternative?

'A policy of kill, torture, expel, degrade Arabs brings us all down. Even if you take angels and get them to force people down, they will become bastards.'

Reuven had all the hard facts at his fingertips: 78% of

Palestine has been taken over, and into the remainder the Israelis are pushing roads and walls to support the 200 'settlements'. All resistance is being looked on as justification for yet more expulsions. The Israelis have gone from hegemonic peace to perpetual war. Amram Mitzna, the general Mayor of Haifa, looked like the 'get-out' front-runner candidate in the Labor Party. His policy was not extreme in itself but it was in effect, in the current situation. 'The Labor Party's tilting to the left in moving away from wanting the Palestinians to remain terrorists. The extreme right does not want that, as peaceful negotiation would theoretically mean compromise.'

He referred to the latest policy of returning to the Zionist/terrorist behaviour of the 1920s onwards: shooting, bombing and demolishing to make life intolerable for villagers. Yahoun, near Nablus, was to be the first place to see the execution of this policy. Reuven believed this action would backfire on Israel.

'Empires extend, then collapse. It's the economy, stupid!' And the near future?

'The attack on Iraq is not a sign of strength, it's weakness. The US has had to increase its hegemony.'

Asked why the Jews of all people should behave in such a repressive manner, he added, 'Between torturing and being tortured it's maybe better not to be tortured, but there are better things to do with your life than to torture.' (quoting Edward Said) 'God forbid to be the victim of a victim.'

We returned to our tourist agenda with a visit to the Mount of Olives. As our driver took us there he showed us where his own village was, down in a valley. At the time the village was shrinking as Israelis bought up properties to build new homes on its edges; an echo of the sneaky but strictly legal way Disney took over farmland for Disney World back in the USA. By 2003, this area, in the midst of Palestinian Jerusalem, could be another fortified 'settlement'.

As we stood looking back down at the Dome of the Rock we were abruptly surrounded by a predatory gang of souvenir hawkers; I tried shouting myself hoarse: 'No no no' but my words were wasted. Sue had seen it all before and did her best to shoo them away. They did fade away after a pestilential while. Then Janet found that her purse, lying on the street when it should have been in her pocket, had been emptied of her money - paper and plastic. I noticed then that all my notes, in an envelope for the post office, had also been grabbed. I tried a rather pointless chase after the crooks, who had become as one with the air, finally rejoined the crestfallen group, who were worriedly calling my name, and seriously blew my cool.

Anyway, we wandered on, stopping to admire the door (locked) leading to the Garden of Gethsemany and crossed back over the valley to the Old City for a last bit of tourist behaviour, including a visit to the copshop for the girls. Sue and I shared some cola at the al-Amoud Gate. I found a tourist-type shop which sold film. The Kodak box was covered with a sticky layer of fine, sooty dust - a testament to the state of the holiday industry in Palestine/Israel.

Later I persuaded John, Janet and Eileen to join me for a last look at the magic of the night. We passed down the lane where, a couple of nights before, I had ineptly got involved in a four-man game of keepie-uppie, our shadows leaping and licking the narrow walls like flames, and to the Square, which at night would do nicely as a stage set for The Nutcracker, although the ambience, it being the third day of Ramadan, was more like Hogmanay; men taking their kids for walks, and boys roaming the streets on foot or roaring around in cars. The party atmosphere continued back at the hotel, where Sue requested a portrait of Achmed. I did my best with a ballpoint on hard, shiny computer paper, but had to work fast, as the model got ants in his pants after a few seconds. His pal also wanted a portrait, and tested my art-school training to its extreme, as his idea of posing was to jump around the lounge, babbling and laughing. The portraits were polished off with flashy signatures.

On our last day, we paid Hanna Nasser, the (Christian) Mayor of Bethlehem, a visit. He welcomed, as all the Palestinians we have met have done, the opportunity to tell all. He started by listing the five incursions recently suffered by the town, the most famous being of course in April 2002, including the siege of the Church of the Nativity. Always under the pretext of chasing 'terrorists'.

'Implementing the UN Resolution is the only way to stop the violence. The settlements are endangering Bethlehem's existence - taking water as well as land, and indiscriminate shooting at Palestinians. The United Kingdom must be involved in implementing the UN Resolution. At the moment, all the compromise is being asked of the Palestinians and none from Israel. Palestinians strongly believe that Palestine's and Israel's future is conjoined and must be seen as mutual. The situation now has caused 65% unemployment. Because of travel restrictions the Palestinian Authority cannot collect taxes. Five million Euros per month are needed for repairs and maintenance - buildings, lights, pavements and trees, after the tank invasion. So far, 1,500 Christians and 2,000 Muslims have left Bethlehem and Beit Jala. We don't want to evacuate town for the Christians, although there is much support from Scandinavia.'

The Mayor, having noticed my accent, mentioned one notable exception in the

less-than-enthusiastic political support from foreign parts: The Glasgow Provost's visit with a delegation twice during the curfew. He planned a job-creation scheme, linking with Glasgow. As just one example of the losses for which the country is still trying to compensate: the Mayor's father lost five houses and five pieces of land in 1948.

'Now things are more dangerous again. With the world's eyes on Iraq and Bush's war, Israel wants to grab the land around Rachel's Tomb. Now "talk of transfer" is against Palestinians who refuse to leave, having survived previous enforced exile, including in 1967, when most of the four local villages were destroyed. There is talk of the Palestinians having a state by 2005, but it's only talk. Netanyahu or Sharon - it's the same money with two faces.'

Mr Nasser mentioned having written to all the churches of the world, but that they are conspicuously silent even though their followers were among those in danger of being disposed. He described Palestine as being divided into four types of area: (1) big cities /West Bank, (2) Palestinian control, (3)Israeli 'security' areas, (4)no one allowed - under full Israeli control.

'Before the Intifada, the GDP was getting healthy and employment was increasing. Then the invasions - October, March, April, June and August. We don't need any more agreements now, or 'projects'. If the resolutions already made were followed it would be enough.'

Over tea and coffee we were shown photos of yet more army destruction, in the apolitical municipal offives. Furniture, files and computers were smashed in the now familiar old routine.

The Mayor himself had trouble with the army. On the 6th February at two a.m. there was a loud knock on the door, answered by his wife who found soldiers shouting and shooting in the air. When he joined her, the soldiers ordered him out of the house. Although they threatened to hit him he said, 'No! You get out of my house! ' They insisted, though, on making him stand on the pavement for over half an hour. 'Why are you doing this?' he demanded. 'We have been informed you are hiding gunmen in your house!'

They didn't leave one house unsearched.

We thanked the Mayor for his time. His final word was, 'We will continue to challenge Israel until we get our home.' He hoped we could bring others next time; so did we.

At the airport it was even stickier leaving than entering. One or two of us got the third degree. A little girl in uniform grimly took me aside and sternly barked questions - when I turned to ask Eileen the name of 'that hotel', the girl got annoyed: 'I am talking to you, not her!'

I hoped that my bow-legged cowboy walk did not draw attention to the New improvised Notes I had stuffed in my underpants. A couple of fancy painted souvenir candles were removed from my bag to the X-ray while I spun a few half-truths. I got carried away with the apparent success of my flannelling and started to chat up

my new interrogator.
A few weeks after our return home, the tanks rolled into Bethlehem, and once again it
was a closed prison camp.

Convoy Three

Ordinary home life gradually blended into this adventure: on the fourth December 2009 a plasterer arrived to finish rendering my new fire surround. He declined my tip & suggested I give it to the Palestinian children. (I had told him where I planned to take my next 'holiday').
I phoned the doc's for result of my recent blood test. No change despite a minor nose-bleed while making love the previous night. I used a regular cocktail of drugs to keep my heart and my brain from seizing up.
I heaved my suitcase & bag up to the street, push walk to footbridge to the town centre. It was taped off by cops! I remembered I forgot my rail-pass, so I got the bus back home including a walk up hill with trolley. From home it was a taxi the long way to the town centre. No big crowd to give us the cheering send-off I had planned to record for my radio show, just a daft brass band combo playing joke-clumsy 'Rawhide' - which made it, of course, into my radio show. Eventually after all the speeches by the councillors & MPs , Barbara Janke, Stephen Williams etc. we started to drift off. Monica revealed we were not travelling to London today. I asked Rowland if it was really true. I allowed myself to be talked into joining the slow drive to Easton Mosque to collect donations for

convoy expenses on the basis of Rowland's offer of a lift home. After my efforts to get to this non-event, I really regressed into 'huffy child': hurt, angry, brattish victim. At the (deserted) mosque I slowly returned to adulthood as the ice-cold sunny day segued into an ice-cold rainy day. Mohamed did his best to jolly me up by pulling my woolly hat down and when that didn't work he grabbed me, my arms pressed against my sides, and lifted me up a couple of times. There's a tiny food market here under the motorway facing the mosque door. Monica and I took our turn to leave the parked lorry, vans, cars and chums collecting for Gaza in buckets, and went for coffee in the local café. It was of the old school: thin, tasteless and boiling hot. But 'hot' was important. Jeremy kindly gave me a lift home - earlier scenarios included leaving my luggage in the van I would be travelling in, and just going ahead to London tonight with Siamak.

Home, warm and dry…

5 December'09:

Three-fortyfive –I woke up, sweating. Body clock worked. Just as well; the alarm clock didn't. My lift with the girls (from Sudan) arrived at five-thirty. We were due at Big Yellow Storage at five. Left for London in the dark and arrived at London Gateway petrol station, car park with coffee machine & newspapers, nine a.m.

Noon - the rest of the convoy joined us, one hour late. We had to sign indemnity forms (assuming we are all of the American persuasion regarding litigation) and agreement forms to allow Viva Palestina to use any 'footage' we might shoot. It's all more complicated because cool, passive Alison and flustered little friend had set up two queues and gave us conflicting instructions: queue here - no - just one rep. per vehicle. No… - I retired. Monica appeared at Tony's van where I sat writing this account, with the forms. After which I had to go and hand over my passport to get a nice VP card. On my advice, Monica and Tony jumped in and we escaped before the rules changed again. A long journey up Gunnersbury Lane to Neasden, to Tony's home near Legoland. His mostess hostess wife Joy cooked up a big meal and he drove me to Sainsbury's to stock up on easy-cook food for the journey ahead. Monica revealed that the info emailed round about gas cookers being disallowed by Eurotunnel, was fiction. Only big ones are out.

Tony and Joy live in a tiny jewel-like modern suburb house, with a spruce tree forest behind, Maurice Sendak style. PVC windows, vinyl wallpaper, fitted carpets and left-wing books - Pilger, Chomsky, Fisk etc.

I noted 'Dead silence outside' - but it was only six a.m. The peace was disturbed by Tony being unable to find his passport. As noon approached and while I ate breakfast, quietly prepared by Joy, Tony continued to search his car and the VP van and all his pockets. Monica joined me and eventually had breakfast too. We three departed for the gathering on the M25. Again arriving much earlier than everyone else. Tony phoned everyone he could. He decided to try to get an emergency passport on Monday and join us again later. Joy drove behind us, and waited with us in the motorway canteen to take Tony back home. Monica planned to get another driver – one with a passport, if she could find one. This would lead to a showdown between her and Sakir over who was in charge.

We picked up boxes of paper en route, from two of Tony's neighbours/fellow Palestine activists, who had a Bert Irvin print on their wall. A long wait again at the gathering then we all drove 30 miles south to another motorway café for an address by organiser Kevin followed by a speech by George Galloway which got our blood racing - something we all needed on a cool, misty morning. He reminded us that we must all now take our time-keeping seriously   - arriving on the 27th, the anniversary of the bombing, would get us in the paper faster than arriving after it's out of the news and Israel is no longer getting bad press - so Egypt might get coverage for delaying us.

Kevin said that not only had many people been late on Saturday, some didn't show up at all; hence delay to the Eurotrain. We heard Siamak, who I'd almost travelled with on Friday – had had a breakdown and hardly got out of Bristol.

I found that during the melée on Saturday (where Tony maybe lost his passport), I should have paid for my Eurotrain passage. I kept notes throughout this journey, and 'write this on the train' approaching La France and perhaps a showdown with the Purser. Despite the little upsets, I was enjoying the journey with little Siba, the multi-lingual good Muslim and mighty fine driver. Her sister who only came to see us off, returned home from the motorway stop. After decanting from the Eurotunnel, we headed to a car park in Belgium via France: Brussels - a kind of suburb which could have been in England. A huge parking lot bordered by distant trees. A crowd of well-wishers welcomed us in the dark. Monica's van, driven by Michael from Ireland, was parked away from the Bristol group. Sakir, who had been complaining about her being bossy, 'hi-jacked' the van, moving it to our area. later when at sleeping time a few of us boys in our van were talking about Monica and laughing , she appeared - said she had been setting up her tent when the van disappeared and took fifteen minutes to find it; she accused Sakir of embarrassing her.

He said to me he just wanted the group to keep together and would prefer not to have to do all this stuff. He was certainly not being diplomatic when he nicked Monica's van - but if he was guilty of bad behaviour so was I, as I was there, too.

It was a freezing night. two or three hours' sleep then disturbed snatches of cold and sleep, in the van's back seat, with a gap exposing my upper legs to an updraft of icy air through my sleep. Without the fisherman's woolly hat over my head I would not have survived. I'm not tough, unlike Siba, who in the cold night air and wind, ritually washed herself with bottled water and prayed as she normally would.

I cooked hot water for coffee in the morning. Tony's forwarded advice about everyone on the road - or travelling in the streets - having to wear max-visibility jackets, was overstated, like the warning against gas stoves.

We had to leave for La Mur, Saarbruken, Stuttgart but stopped twenty minutes out for one van to get diesel. The stop extended to three hours as people shopped, ate, hung out, got lost. All on one tiny service station. The mounting frustration won at last as we left, two thirty local time.

Monica gave me some vitamin tabs and chatted to Siba about the CB phone frequency. I hoped Sakir would make an effort to cross the gap too, but I needn't have worried: he announced over CB that we will have a special meal at the Stuttgart Hilton - 20 Euros per head.

By the time I got back from the WC)á bientot) this had taken on a life of its own. It was now the Hilton Bikeshed. Siba found a crazy local radio station on the van radio, 'le son' -techno dance. We drove under a flashing sign:
pas de fete
sans bob

Passed through fabulous industrial area: gigantic floodlit towers, chimneys, dark and shiny. Ending up at a truck park near Ostildren, our van in the midst of this expanse called Carl-Zeiss-Strasse. I cooked myself tinned veg curry between vans, away from the wind. In the shadows a fellow-traveller stumbled on my tiny cooker as soon as the flame went out, half-destroying it. 'Oh! Sorry!' 'Okay...'

As I looked for water Sakir took over our wheel. He, I , Siba and Mohammed (a big, Syrian all-American boy who lives in Turkey) headed towards town, looking for piss-haus and eatery. We found the first and parked Siba there. Continuing late, but it was weirdly quiet for all that - This little town we found - a new replica of an old village, with a shiny new main strasse, had absolutely no spark of life. Joining up again, we continued our mystery tour of edge of Stuttgart looking for an open shop with a toilet. We found a shop - no - better - it was what Mohammed wanted: a burger stall, in centrum. I bought some snacks and nipped into the back to brush my teeth and empty my bladder. We got lost finding our way back, circling round the dark, mysterious German industrial cityscape and got back at two.

First thing in the morning I lost a lens out of my glasses. It was in the van, but irretrievably lost. By the time Siba woke I gave up looking and took the short walk to the corner shop for kaffé. It was open. Excellent! I continued to write as normal but it was difficult, quarter-eyed. I wasn't alone in my troubles: since the previous day, Siba had been suffering a dreadful back/arm pain, maybe from driving. I gave her Paracetamol. She claimed to feel better. Another sign we passed pointed to a side road:

Wierde

Over coffee I heard the Rumour Circuit news: Tony found his passport. It was in his car. He and Siamak were to join us on the road near the Alps just inside Switzerland.

At 2.20 Siomak arrived. We were all gathered in the blue shadow of the mountains, for the night. I could relax, after Sakir ordered me to. Monica was upset because she followed Tony to help him erect his tent but he ran off. He appeared at my table right after and wondered why she was annoyed. " Oh no, I'm not camping! I'm sleeping in the back of the van."

'Ah,' I replied, 'That's how it starts. You said *drink*,' (he was just opening a can) 'she heard *tent*.'

I noted: "We've been in this kaffe haus for an eternity. I was aghast, thinking it might be 10.00. I could go out to the minibus for a kip but I'm buzzing from the adrenaline. Regret I didn't bring my laptop as many others have - I will have a hugely piledin-tray to deal with on my return.

I'm getting very 'ultra real' visuals increasing in sparkiness. In the book I'm reading, the word "got" looks out of place, foreign and in danger of floating off.

Early to bed for most of us. Siba wants to hit it at 11.00. I go too. in my sleeping-bag on the front seat.

I wake at five - too cold to sleep! Go back into the café, park my arse on a high-stool and get out my book. It becomes **9 December'09**.'

Our big plan to leave at the crack of seven got elasticated - Siba surfaced and drove me to our rendezvous with Sakir across the motorway. As we moved I realised that my padded car-coat, without which I was doomed to frozen death in my sleep, was still in the kaffe haus. I begged Siba to return; she said it's OK as we are doubling back anyway. The routine, known only to the drivers(which I'd assumed would be a straight-forward on-to-the-road) seemed to involve returning to the eatery, which we did, after which I put out an SOS on the CB radio about my lost property. As Siba pulled into the car park, I opened the door and jumped out. This freaked her out as she saw it as dangerous. Our leader was out there with my coat! I gave him a hug in exchange. Siba disappeared for a while. Siamak appeared, all jollification and ebullience, suggesting I might like to join him in his van as I like music. Not so warm as Siba's but good! I said 'I'm happy where I am, but thanks.' (What became of our early start?) - Then the girl reappeared, and was surprised to see I wasn't with Siamak. I got the feeling I would have to keep my head down.

Later we heard she had got the news that she had just split with her boyfriend, so she could have been happier.

Onwards! As usual the heat was up full to compensate for Siba's cold feet, or maybe peripheral neuropathy. I discovered that my sense of geography was seriously at fault. We were in Austria, not Switzerland. We got a good look at the Alps, which of course were fabulous and Siba wanted me to video her driving with them as the backdrop.

Emergency stop just inside Italy - we saw smoke coming from number 6's exhaust. It took a good while to fix, so we all found something to eat; I found the shop would sell me a pair of cheap glasses, and wrote two letters. Finally the long haul got to Modena. The convoy parked under floodlights at the entrance to a café/restaurant/toilet stop, looked really big. After an ill-advised last coffee I bedded down at eleven, same as Siba, with my gloves and woolly hat on. Five past three: woke needing a piss and feeling the cold. I went out, did my thing, got back, lay down for an hour. It was hopeless! And I was shivering. Back to the all-night café. Finally I stood at the high table, writing, as Thursday approached. 'Don't forget the snowman!' I wrote. During our stop on the border someone started to build a Palestinian snowman. As we stood back to admire the finished 'man' with his red, black and green scarf, Siba's in-van CD of Koran readings set to music seemed to be echoing off the high blue mountains surrounding us....

The toilets in Austria were expensive but spotlessly clean and dry. A haven. In stark contrast, they are free in Italia, but not clean and in our first morning all bogs were flooded. I gingerly lined the top of one (no seat) with paper and balanced my reading book on the cambered top of the cistern part, praying that it wouldn't fall off into the flood. Success! I had a good shit, but my pen fell into the piss water. <u>This</u> pen. We drove through the upcoming sun to Rimini. Stopped there by the sea.

The front was all huge art-deco hotels and pleasure beach, laid out for promenading. All the guys (and a couple of the girls) played volleyball for a good while; I didn't. I posted a postcard, looked at the sand, architecture, blueness and white. We all went in search of pizza. I doubled back to decant my drugs and plane ticket into one bag to take with me rather than leave it in Siamak's permanently unlocked van. I joined some of the team in the only café open, for a microwave lasagne (five euros) I learned that Siamak usually climbs up back on top of his packed toys etc. and that if I tried sleeping on the seat I would get his foot in my face in the night if he climbed down to exit (he can't get out of the back) - so I would have to get the tent up after all.

Our long drive to Ancona was waylaid by number 3 in our mini-convoy, driven by Tony, taking the wrong turn. Of his leaders, he said, 'They just disappeared!'

Not playing the game, and unfair to Tony. It happens. So we took the local road instead of the motorway, which we eventually found by doubling back a few times (and seeing some Italian small-town life instead of the industrial and warehouse motorway surroundings.)

Ancona is built on several steep and closely crowded hills, its streets tottering up several ways, and at the upper parts are old houses and almost entire original old streets - but it looks as if it were built since 1965. We got lost many times trying to find our next tryst but I found it fascinating although frustrating as everyone around me tried to keep from getting seriously pissed off. Against all odds we ended in a huge deserted, gently sloping factory ground - not quite the edge-of-town 'arena' we were being told to go for. Just what went wrong has to remain a mystery.

The tribe was all there! Ambulances, vans, the Big One. People cooking, tents erected. It was dark but still only eight thirty. As I took in the little group of travellers with a cartoon-cloud balloon of campfire smoke floating above and lit by the floodlights like a suspended ectoplasm of our communal presence, I had a strong feeling of togetherness, of camaraderie and a feeling that being like this, on the road, was being in the right place, and that it was how I would like it to always be.

Gradually I got used to the night surroundings - the star light and the tall floodlights on our heads took over - but especially the stars above the elegant rows of office-like buildings that appeared to have faces at their tops. They were ranged in a majestic curve, looking down over the railway line at the bottom of the slope. The occasional roar of a distantly passing car became relaxing, like sea waves. I looked really hard at the distant tall buildings, split by the streets and down-lit by the stars, the row of square eyes along their top floors benevolently looking down - and at the sky, to keep it all in. I got out my tent for its maiden erection, with no idea of its size. The obvious place to do this would be on a sunny day in your own well-tended garden. Not the old car-park in an abandoned factory at night. We were surrounded by wasteland, landscaped greenery and farther uphill, even farmland, ploughed fields hanging downhill like throws on a couch. It was dark. And very cold. I made some cursory attempts at assembling the tent on a tiny grassy island in the tarmac/concrete; I realised this is crazy, with a '!' - I rolled it up as well as I could - no chance of getting it as tightly rolled as it was back into the little bag made for it - I made for Siamak's van, hoping to find someone who could give me a hand - but I saw Monica bustling towards me; she asked 'What's up?'

'It's the first time I've tried this. It's gonna take me some time to get it figured out.'

Monica went into 'mother' mode, insisting that I join her to find a bigger grass patch and do the tent. Okay - and she did practically all of the work, as the basic design had similarities to her own tent. Not only that - she insisted on lending me a blanket. Sakir appeared, looking worried - suggested I wait until Greece or Syria to try the tent. I could sleep in the big lorry! But as it was up I decided to carry on - just for one night at least. It was bigger than I needed - enough room for four people - if they really liked each other. I slept really well. At five a.m. I woke for the long walk across the sloping, cracked concrete expanse and a dead road to the bushes near the railway for a piss. I could see the stars so much more clearly than in the UK, even though we were near a city. Miraculously I got back to sleep.

11December'09

I managed to get my tent collapsed and rolled up in less than twenty minutes. Being nylon, it was wet outside (nature) and damp inside (me), but although everything was a little damp, it was the best sleep I'd had so far. We left early - genuinely early for once, to find our way through Ancona to the docks. This was old Ancona - mostly bare bricks unadorned with render or paint. Three hours in the booking office, a scene straight from Emigrants in, say, 1890.Partly complicated by there being so many of us at once, and partly by the options being offered. Just travel, or have or share a cabin (shower!) which you could share with three others although there were only two bunks, so two would sleep, not strictly kosher, on the floor, but all three would get a wash. In the end I settled for being dirty, and snoozing (I hoped) in the lounge. As we set sail to Greece, I noted 'So far I've put £41.05 in the road tax machines and given Sakir E.200 for general expenses, plus E.100 for this 'cruise' in the Adriatic Sea.' I was surrounded by guys who were much more into an incredibly stupid sitcom on Italian TV than staring at the sea, which they had seen before. I, having had a shit, followed by coffee and cake, stared at the sea. The sky, viewed from the top deck, was fabuloso; the weather being of the kind that would guarantee spectacularly clear skies. I tried recharging my mobile with my solar recharger, but leaving it on top of Siba's dashboard, which often got to be suitable for frying eggs, had left it a little bit dead. I discovered that there were showers, probably because there was an outdoor swimming pool on the top deck. I gladly seized the opportunity to nail the pong that I suspected I was carrying. As I came back out, the setting sun laid on a big show.

  Our branch leader, Sakil, appeared with a few cohorts, followed by others. There was to be a meeting of all on the top deck. What we had done so far, special mentions for some, an apology for the last-minute substitution of that wasteland for the 'arena' in Rimini hardly needed as I told Kevin, remembering my floatation towards satori. And the timetable and trials to come. An English kid got up and gave a rabble-rousing speech which suggested that the Palestinians may be able to do more for us than we can do for them. 'Don't talk about going to Gaza. It was there before you were born, and it will be there after you are gone. It is up to each and everyone of you to make your own connection, and it's not just to help yourself. You must have your own reason to be there - and it's not just to help yourself. It's up to you to make of it, of this journey, what you can, for the people of Gaza.'

Shouts of 'right-on' in Arabic all round.

I was sorry I hadn't recorded him, but my stomach dictated a look for another capuccino and bar sandwich for my Tea. The ship was obviously a posh cruiser rather than a "MacBrayne's ferry": chaps in liveried costumes striding about tidying up but it was OK for the passengers to be sleeping rough. The deal seemed to be that this is chartered, so it's our home and we can kip as we like. I couldn't liberate my sleeping-bag from the van as the garage decks were closed for the journey, but it was plenty warm in the lounge. At six-thirty, still noisy from the TV. I read my book until sleepy enough to sleep - this came at twelve-thirty. It was quieter, but the late-night Euorotrash TV soldiered on and the unused fruit machines before me (this little area being the'casino')occasionally bleated their particular bleats. We were heading for Verria, near Thessaloniki. I had to run round the two garage decks to find Siamak's van for disembarking. Eventually as I got a lift from two helpful fellows with an ambulance I discovered he was first off.

The convoy drove away up into the lair of the gods. It was snowy and got colder again as we aimed for Thessaloniki through an unprecedented number of tunnels, some very long indeed, and forever rising higher into the clouds. Snow, fog, sleet; and as we finally descended, rain. Every time we came out of a tunnel we were hit by another astounding mountain scene. Siba cooed out over the CB about some little dogs by the road.

'So cute!' Francis suggested that they were bears. Everyone piled into the controversy which was resolved when we stopped at a café/shop. It was two Alsation types, sitting by the petrol pumps. Closer, we could see they were in fact a family - a dozen adolescent puppies and maybe an aunt too. They all crowded round Mohammed, who crouched down feeding them crispy snacks in the wet.

Onwards. We stop outside the city, at the police offices building. By the side of the motorway to assemble the entire convoy for a big entrance. My guess was that Kevin (who was running the whole show) had somehow organised this with the cops. We waited.

The convoy entered Thessaloniki, and during our tortuous crawl through the narrow suburbanite main streets, C12 ahead of us Siamak lost the leaders and we got lost again. Three rounds, or more, of this part of the city. Not as fascinating as the previous lost experiences. But pretty in parts. Eventually we reached a hill overlooking town, where we parked in mud and grass behind the basketball arena. Tea and sandwiches had been laid on. It was plenty warm inside too - very welcome as Greece this far north in December is freezing. The clamber down the hill-side of unkempt grass, bushes and clay, was worth it. There were toilets of the most basic variety. Cludges with no seats, cold water, wet floor. Better than shitting in the bushes, perhaps. Kevin had warned us all that from now on, toilet paper would have to be dropped into a bin instead of being flushed. After our grub and the talk and questions, half of us too over the court for some free-form ball games. I was impressed by a little French girl who could run round the court bouncing the ball as she ran, so that it looked like being attached loosely to her by magnetism. I was entranced - no way I could break in there. She was well advanced. When I picked up a couple of stray balls to chuck them back in, I made a fine mess of just that simple act. It was bad enough when I was a kid! The playing went on till nine pm…

Kostas Theodorikas, The Mayor of the principality, who was giving us a 'proper meal', appeared with a few politicians, including two MPs and an embarrassed interpreter who was clearly unused to public speaking, and very deferential. They joined our man Kevin behind a row of plastic tables set up with the Palestinian flag along the front. Speeches of welcome and good wishes were made. Then we ate. Boiled eggs, feta cheese, fancy bread, apples.

More charging around the court for the sporty types, and finally it was bed time, and we were invited to sleep in the arena.

13 December'09

I woke, six forty-five. It had cooled down in the hall. But warm compared to outside: drizzly and freezing, overcast. It was our 'day off'. We were expected to leave the arena by nine - at eight-fortyfive some lazy buggers were still in their sleeping bags, ignoring the 'badom badom badom' ball-bouncing which started again around eight thirty a.m. Accompanied by the shouts and bangs of the convoy boys chucking themselves around the floor of this small arena, Sakir, a little stiff and serious, took me aside and said I've to travel in one of our mini-vans from now on. 'They're our mini-buses, and no-one can take them away from us. No-one can deny us the right to travel in them.' I mentioned the rumour that he would no longer be driving the big lorry. He said he just wanted 'to get into Gaza. I'm no hero. I've been there already, and I don't have to make a point. But if the bloke who takes it over, it took six months of my life to get the bloody thing together, if he leaves it there, whoever he is, I'll stick one on him.'

Had someone tried to kick him out? 'They're mixing things.' – (He had been disagreeing with the IHH people – and Samak, about the fate of our vehicles, which had never been settled.) 'Are they?' I asked.

'These things don't belong to us and we shouldn't treat them like we do'

Monica appeared and said since Sakir said whatever he said, 'Siamak's not a journalist, writer and only a driver, he felt at a loss. He had suggested that if he is not to be a driver' (I don't know if Sakir or 'they' told him that) 'He wants to go home, his flight paid by Viva Palestina.'

Monica and I agreed that Sakir had been a little melodramatic in stating that he's resigning in response to whatever 'They' said. Later, over our free (thanks to the mayor) food, Monica and I agreed that Sakir is a man who just basically enjoys a good huff, and that we shouldn't separate him from his indulgence. She had told him that she would tell the Turks to respect the work the Brits had put into the Convoy and the transport, and let them finish the drive to the end. He had vaguely waved assent without a lot of enthusiasm. We two decided to leave everything as it was and continue on the assumption that that is pink and fluffy.

……

Eleven-thirty a.m: The convoy, with police escort, winded down into town, assailed on the way by happy men, women and children waving and sticking up victory signs. All the dogs came to look, too. We parked in a half-mile line on the waterfront. Sunday afternoon in Saloniki is Friday night everywhere else. The cool and groovy were out promenading and families on foot or in cars cruising the one-way front were mixing and the city was exchanging its life-blood all over. We did a lot of banner-waving and sloganising for cameras, movie and still, and some of us climbed to the roof of the White Tower to wave the Palestinian and Greek flags. The Tower, a one-time jail, is a fascinating museum. I strolled off for coffee in one of the front cafés. A large black. First in 24 hours; it tasted gorgeous. They added in a free cake, and I got a grandstand view of a big yacht race coming in. Back to the van to arrange a rendezvouz with Siamak. He wanted to go to a wi-fi café. I guessed this was cool.. As long as I got coffee. We found a noisy dark hole full of computers and no coffee. I left him to it and wandered off through the old city, finding by accident its historical remnants. To the north, like burst pustules in the skin of the city, holes of a great many sizes and shapes allowed ancient remains of the Turks and Romans to sit with their heads sticking up into the future. Some times it's only a column or two exposed, sometimes an entire church or the frontal edifice of something unimaginably huge.

    My return to the wi-fi for Siamak was pointless - he was deeply embroiled in sending back photos to the BG Link website - couldn't come out to play. I was off again. I ouldn't find my way back to the ancients, but stumbled into the narrow back streets near the docks, full of stalls, cafés, tiny shops, crumbling old houses. The area seems endless. It was quiet, being Sunday afternoon, but I could see the possibilities. Soho, expanded to the size of the City of London.

I missed my lift back from Siamak so I got in a van driven by Algerian Mustapha, who was waiting for his late pal. We looked for him and found him with friends of a similar bent, in a noisy wi-fi- bar. He didn't want to leave, so we were off. To get lost in many fascinating ways. Not helped by my writing the name of our destination "polychini" on the back of my hand and then reading it as "polychai" when asking locals for directions.

The really funny thing is when I discovered Tony and Monica following us, mistaking Mustapha's el zoomo driving for confidence. They must have been circling around for hours.

14 December'09

Breakfast in a local café with Siamak, Christian and his tent-mate Francis, the documentarist who's filming the trip. Francis looks Chinese or Mongolese but speaks Australian. His mother is Chinese.

I slept all the way to Kabala. I got a full night's sleep first, so for a change I was not buzzing with adrenalin. We ate at a new 'ticket office' café on the waterfront. It was an icy wind outside. On to Alexandropoulis. The front three of the convoy turned off; the rest of us kept on. I'm not sure which of us was right. "we" being the SW England grouping. But the majority travelled on for maybe 20 miles, turning off to farmland, little share crops, houses, chickens, the ubiquitous roadside mini-altars. Miraculously we joined together with the other three and all drove down to the seaside in time for a big peaceful, balmy orange sunset. The gentle waves making a 'doppler' effect sound as they washed up. We could almost camp here - but after taking photos of each other and the sea and sun and enjoying the peaceful gentleness of the shore, we headed back out into Alexandropoulis.

Our destination was theAlexandropoulis campsite, well out of town. No cafés or shops. Dark. Drear.

But after we all parked, Siamak took one, two then three of Siba's matches and got a tiny pile of leaves to burn. We all, Siba, Francis, Christian, added twigs, then logs. Francis found a wood palette. We had a blazing campfire. The night was transformed. Tony and Monica should have been with us but they were parked elsewhere in the trees on this vast site. By the time I got back from the showers (hot water exists in Greece after all -a first) Siba had found chairs from the out-of-season-closed-site-café and Siamak, keeping in touch with Mohamed in Bristol via his blueberry, could announce the news: Sakir, who had been conspicuously absent from the trip for 24 hours (although the entire convoy was at the camp) had, surprisingly, driven off his big baby and entered Turkey.

Our evening round the fire went on till eleven forty-five although the 'stoned' effect of cooking our faces and the psychological comfort effect of the glow made us sleepy at seven-thirty. It was Big Fun; funny stories, Siamak's guitar being plunked by Christian, altogether a feeling of being happily linked. Siamak and I decided on behalf of us all that we would welcome Sakir back as a member of the group, bearing in mind whatever stories he's been giving them. Siamak told me Sakir had said something about not wanting to be a group leader any more - not with this group. Sakir had confided in me only that he didn't want to be group leader.

Francis and Christian told us all that they had

become such good tent buddies they'll have some explaining to do to their wives.

Kevin's pep-talk warned us we may need loads of money for Turkish visas. I missed most of his talk while queuing for the only three male bogs open.

Hit the road! Skirting the city's edge for the motorway - rain and fog.

In the queue at the border, we noticed an army vehicle dugout on the Greek side, old camouflage netting half-covering its drive down entrance. At the border we got visas (E15), changed money & ate, mostly ignoring the duty-free trash, then proceeded to the Turkish entrance where I quietly added a voice-over to my recording of the approach to the gate beyond which is a huge crowd waving banners and cheering. My voice-over was trashed by the customs officer's taking exception to his Greek counterpart not having stamped my passport <u>twice</u>. It took nearly half an hour to find the Greek stamper and get him back to his little concrete box. We at last got through, Siamak and I, having missed the crowd but still got plenty of well-wishers in anoraks but some in their best, like the young guy who gave me a Turkish flag on a stick, in his finest shiny suit. Despite the biting wind. All through Turkey we passed little groups of welcomers. Occasionally with special one-off welcome banners.

During a piss-stop Siamak left me to guard his stuff in the unlockable van. He was longer than I expected – being the kind of guy he is, he spent time greeting people while he was out, and I started to think I would like to go, too. I hid my microphone in the trash on the floor - bags, fruit from the Turks, old wrappers, and was about to make a sprint for it when he returned with Francis, who was hot to get moving. Anyway, we were off. As we drove, I couldn't find my mic and started rummaging about for it. Danger alert! Bad noise! Van not accelerating properly! After a few words with others by CB Siamak parked for a look. I jumped out, mostly to see where my mic was. In the rubbish bag, which had fallen down to the door step. The mic, unseen I guess, had fallen out of the door and rolled under the van to be left as we pulled out.

Incidentally, Sakir reappeared at the border control. he caught up with the convoy in time to see Huge Noisy Crowd of people and cars, a traffic jam - an 'official welcome' - flashing lights & hooting horns outside Istanbul. I didn't realise it was Istanbul until we got through.

A long, long ride through the city, over the water way down to the southern parts, for a big meal laid on by the mayor at the polished restaurant in a park. Thankfully a short speech followed by others including two American orthodox rabbis. We left and were guided to somewhere else - it transpired that we were not in fact camping here. Great having all this organised, but at the time I would have liked to know what was going on. To another sports auditorium: Ismek Beykoz - We would be given breakfast after kipping on their warm floor - and the girls got their own room this time. (Breakfast out in Greece was given free to us convoy boys) But as I scribbled and others drank their tea, I reflected on having to get a lift here, with Iqbal and husband, while my luggage came in another van as Siamak's van was not running. And Siba told me she had no idea if <u>she</u> ould have a van next day - she then went to Sakir to discuss something. During the night, two a.m., several guys got up, strode across the floor - I felt every step - with their shoes on, then have a confab in the centre of the 'pitch', then strode away again, some going to reception upstairs and I heard them continue to blabber as three p.m. passed and sleep overcame me. There was also a full meeting somewhere which I missed - to deal with unease at the suggestion the (IHH) Turks take over half of our vans. It was agreed to take them on board, sharing driving. I woke properly at six. Cuppa tea at reception. Iqbal and her husband were there already playing with their laptop.

16 December'09

After a hurried breakfast of cheese, boiled egg, bread, not enough time for jam, we all went to Feshane, upper Bosphorus, old city side. For a press conference with George Galloway. Lots of hanging about, locals mixing, scarves and hats bought or given, flags given, snacks sold, TV crews getting soundbites from George and others. The rain held off till we packed it in. Sakir told me to come to him if there's any trouble, if 'they' give me any problems. 'Who are 'they',?' I asked. 'Just come to me.'

Later I gave him a task: looking out for a mobile phone shop so I can get a charger. I also told him about one piece of trouble we had had - when two of the guys ' wanted to go for a hookah, Siba freaked out, - she wasn't at all interested in 'hookers'. Sakir straightened up, demanded 'What? What guys? Who?'

'Christian, Francis. You got it wrong, too,' I laughed, punching his arm.

Next: a tour of the city for PR, not for fun, alas, so I wouldn't get to see Hagia Sofia and the Hotel Gulhane and pudding shop.

The tour was strictly by main road and freeway - no one might see us, and we see no one. Via Eyup car park - Okmeydani - Levent - Hacrosman - Besiktas - Minonu - Hagia Sofia for one hour free. I found the pudding shop - still there after forty years! Now called The Pudding Shop. I had chocolate - my favourite in 1968, and Turkish coffee. In the next-door café where I and Sheila and our gang went in the old days. I couldn't find the Gulhane or New Gulhane hotels - where we hippies could bed on the roof for pennies long ago – if they were no longer in business, the memory is good enough. Then we returned to the car park for unexpected prepared rolls and buttermilk in the rain and wind. We were told to go away and amuse ourselves for a while, so I with Monica, Adriano (from manhattan) and Omar (Glasgow) went for coffee in the local market, on me. Met the girl in charge of the Turkish contingent - Nalam - our return journey took ten minutes - the outward journey took two hours - a dreadful waste of our free time, I thought, grumpy as usual, and of diesel.

On return to the park we were told that the bus taking us all to Taksim Square for a demonstration (in this heavy rain?) left at seven, and we should find something to do until then. Monica and I wandered off again, for a cup of tea. Didn't get the tea, but I found a car-bound phone charger! On our return we found the bus had left. Tony asleep in the van. We sat in the dark, waiting for everyone's return at ten-fifty - maybe. I ran out in the rain for a piss and bought Toblerone at a stall for all to cheer us up. But even after the Big Regroup we had to wait until eleven fifty-six to get out. Slowly then, so slow we were practically immobile, moving towards the park gate behind six other convoy vehicles. Shakil appeared with news - we were waiting for a police escort.

Twelve-twenty - Tiz appeared with news that our

destination - the sleeping and eating place - was not just out in the suburbs - it was now 160k away. And we ate Tea at four in the morning? Tiz and Ingrid were dancing madly in the rain, having gone past despair to Madness. If we had been told of this long trip earlier we would have been able to organise our own food. I would have something more substantial than Toblerone.

And thoughts about the afternoon trip: people did in fact see us. - maybe it was worth it. Twelve thirty-five - we moved out, arriving at mystery town three-fifty, told to get out of vehicles and carry bedding into Lutfu Yaman Stadium - our drivers then took their vehicles to park elsewhere. We were served by kindly, local volunteers - rice, meat, meat-stuffed bread, water. I was off to lay out my bedding in the arena. Maybe fifty guys were already established and trying to sleep, last thing I remember is my watch said four-thirty. The next day - Thursday - **17 December'09** - was dreich again.

Wakey wakey! Seven-fifteen - more volunteers gave us all breakfast & packed sandwiches. Lots of the travellers didn't arrive when an English-speaker was handy to tell them to get off so they ended at the parking lot, miles away and had to wait for buses back to the arena. They got even less sleep than I did. But all this - the hall, the volunteers, food, buses, must have taken a lot of long-past planning -we should have known more about it at our end. (no police escort - as if we needed one in the late night)

Tony could only see it from his point-of-view. We have been severely inconvenienced; it's all a planning disaster.

Certainly it was disorganised that we were given conflicting accounts (or none) of what was in store. The 'program'stated:'23.00 departure from Taksim to Adapaqzari, dinner in Dapazari & night stay in stadium.'

But we had been told we were going to a suburb. Adapazari is a town - if the distinction matters.

Discovering the local market area, though, a jumble of narrow streets, shops, stalls, mosques. Quite like the old city down river, was a major bonus, and I especially enjoyed the traditional wood buildings held together apparently by cobwebs.

|As we left we were surrounded by yet more locals - men in suits, women in scarves and gowns, giving us happy waves and V signs. Heading for Ankara with 'welcome' and city tour to come.

We were three hours late, with a forty-five minute stop en-route at a motorway café where the crowd gave us all red roses, and we got in some minimal shopping and tea, then straight now to a giant sports stadium to be met by another welcoming crowd with giant banner. Inside: a traditional Turkish bombastic drum and trumpet performance ending in fireworks and a shower of confetti from the roof. During the show, I seated in the V.I,P. seats (why not) was interviewed for TV. We were fed. Lots of bread of course, big rolls full of meat; salad and buttermilk. Monica and I gave Tony time to "recharge his batteries", then we joined the final launch leaving for our next stop: Konye. A long way - arrival at midnight. From what I could see, Konye is a slightly bleak waste with huge high-rise tower blocks separated by vast spaces, not unlike Glasgow's Gorbals area or a workers' community in Siberia. I was offered, by mime, a choice of food or sleep. I chose the second. Midnight is not my favourite time for Tea.

The morning's takeaway consisted mostly of a

traditional meat-stuffed paratha.

18 December'09 Friday

Sunny - the town was on a plain, surrounded by beautiful hills, lit up by the rising sun, the orange clouds and blue sky colliding with the purple of the land in between rolling banks of fog. I join Iqbal and her husband at the serve-yourself laid-on breakfast on the top floor of the stadium. We slept in the basement changing rooms or activity rooms.

Iqbal's a sparky wee Indian, her husband boyishly grave, always introduced as 'my husband'.

I had a major nosebleed in the morning. It stopped eventually.

the day's agenda included another 'tour' - like Istanbul, this was going to be a bomb around the peripheral main roads, waving at the populace. It wound through local streets this time. Just our end of town - the oldest parts being circa 1965. There is probably an old part, <u>really</u> old, somewhere.

We passed a few tiny old one-storey houses cowering in the shadows of the hi-rise blocks that have formed into streets, on our way to a square where local Palestine supporters had gathered to hear big nobs speak from a bus top, and the trad drums &horn band started it off with a bang. My hands shaken by many locals. I felt sorry I couldn't thank them in their own language. After the demo I sat in the van, listening to Tony and Monica squabbling like an old married couple. We ate some of the free food we'd been collecting, while waiting for the rest of the convoy, which had wandered off.

T & M were in an internet café during the demo. Monica said she had a real coffee but it was expensive. I say, if she can tell me where she got it, I promised to buy her another one. This was Turkey, but I hadn't had a decent coffee for almost two days; Instant in the stadium and genuine nescafé on the motorway.

After waiting for about an hour here, one of our fellow vans, driven by Tim, moved off and we followed, assuming Tim knew where he's going. Yes! It was another car park, attached to a mosque, where we were all being fed again by the Turks, who had set up a stall and dispensed rice, meat, water, buttermilk and lots more bread. The others would have been on the scheduled city tour, bigger than our journey to the demo. After resting there was more sitting about in vehicles as the word of the Prophet was sung from the minaret speaker system. Our wait allowed the street urchins to clamber round our doors and reach in through our open windows, to grab like monkeys any flags, food or flowers they hadn't got by begging. We left at two-thirty - the road out passed several ancient communities of crumbly but brightly painted one-storey houses and shacks, mostly only ribbons along the road but the final one has dusty roads leading away backwards into the plain. 'What a relief!' I said, 'So this place has a history after all.'

Monica said, 'What?'

I repeated myself.

'A history?'
'Yes - the village we've just passed.'
'What of it?'
'It's old.'
'Why are you telling me this?'
'I thought you might be interested,' I replied brightly

By this time my new store-bought glasses had broken in two. 'I write this without them, just paid 68 Lira for diesel. My shot - we're all having goes at paying, so no-one has a big shock when the day of reckoning comes.'

Our long journey to Adana ended five minutes before the scheduled time of nine but after waiting for a police escort into town and again to the actual sports arena (another one) we got in at nine-fifty.

Big welcoming crowd in the heavy rain - a helpful guy grabbed my luggage after we parked and walked to the entrance, and he carried it into the hall. The routine was to sit at a table anywhere in this vast space , carpeted and walls hung in black - red carpets leading in from the doors - and one of the friendly ladies in headscarves would bring us polystyrene multiplates of chicken, rice, sauce and cakes. And buttermilk, bottled water and not least, bread.

Bedding was sprouting along the wall on the side of the hall where the lighting was dimmer. Some guys were trying to sleep, but there was so much noise and bustle - even kids of 10 or less running about - that it looked a little premature. Laptops were being brought out and studied. Some of our folks only now began eating. The Muslim brothers were up and assembled in a row for their prayer… Monica was grumbling at Iqbal's insistence on sleeping with the lights on (in the women's room) in case they bumped into the Muslim brothers. This leaves a few questions hanging in the air.

I got back to sleep, had a nice dream then woke properly at six with a mild headache. Had a cuppa chai. There was a stall set up, apparently all-night. Lots of local guys sitting talking and drinking tea. It was assumed I would want sugar - a plastic spoon was chucked into my plastic cup and the cubes were gestured at. The guy was surprised when I Said, No Thanks. I grabbed a chair at one of the long tables and began scribbling again.

'It was slowly getting light outside. A grinning boy, more awake than I felt, who I met the before, who asked my name and country, reappeared at the table and asked. 'Is okay, sit here?'

'Yes,' I said, and obsessively kept on writing. 'Adana stadium is unlike the others we stayed in - no seating. no 'pitch' - just a great big architect-designed box like a hangar with admin and toilets added at the front.

We leave via a 'city tour' at 10.00. I suspect that I have a cold.'

Francis, stuck with being the new accountant, came up with a crackpot 'scheme' where each of us must give him 83 Turkish Lira in money and/or diesel receipts, as 83, an arbitrary sum, is difficult to conjure up or down. Monica Tony, I and Francis agreed that each vehicle should sort out its own spend not spend among its inhabitants and present Francis with the result. I couldn't guess at where this would get us, but by eleven I was getting irritated by the hanging about. Fine for the Turks and laid-back English west-country folk. But it didn't suit me. I've always been like this: back-packing in the 'sixties, I would pass on the chance to visit local relics, museums or just cafés, in case I missed the Big Lift; always all-or-nothing. Finally we left for Gaziantep via the grand tour. We were accompanied by the new arrivals/ additions of actual Turks, including a dump truck for Gaza, plus lots of cars stuffed with families, girls, children waving flags and the usual V signs. Everyone who had a hooter hooted, and all the ambulance sirens were shrieking. Apart from the huge crowds of well-wishers in the streets and jamming balconies, I was struck dumb with overawed wonder at street after street of elegantly and fancifully constructed 'deco' hi-rise apartment blocks, all painted or finished in fabulous colours accentuating the lines of their designs, and a few even plastered with mosaic. It was a Fifth Avenue forest.

As we got out of town my queasiness showed itself as stomach upset. I spent most of our journey sleeping and at our one stop passed on the coffee opportunity, settling instead for water and paracetamol from Monica, Rennies from Tony.

By the time we got to Gaziantep I was startled by the experience of us being welcomed at a big banquet for Palestine in a brightly-lit hall resembling a Muslim bingo club. Many of the family members came this far just for the big do, and would then go home. As we escaped from the bright lights, big noise, Tony insisted on finding an internet café instead of following the others, as he felt confident that a building on the hill was the stadium where we were to stay the night. As he, Monica and I stood about we were accosted by three twenty-ish guys, who wanted to know all about us, exchange names etc. Tony wanted them to guide us to a café. He and Monica, in fractured Arabic, get them to take us. I wasn't not that keen - what on earth did these boys want?

It turned out that we did find a room - and they helped us with our typing; not easy at first as it was a Turkish alphabet and keyboard. Tony got really annoyed, as if he'd paid for a service they couldn't provide. My two companions let the boys ride with us as we looked for the stadium, which turned out to not have been where Tony thought. Unfair!

My unease with these with these kids was quickly evaporating, and I heartily shook their hands as we left - and <u>they</u> paid the bill.

But it was cool. More hand shaking all round as the convoy, or part of it, appeared out of the night and we were able to follow to the new stadium, a more local kind of place - two arenas for the guys to use and one for the gals. I copped a shower in the crudely set-up shower-room, managing to get my clothes a bit wet too. The arena was covered with a nice carpet and bizarrely lit by a row of floodlights as big as toplights. It was only 8.00 but felt later. At home I would be happy to be up and about; here I was surrounded by gesticulating, chattering groups of men and others strolling about as they bark into their mobiles, I was glad I wasn't not the only one copping out of activity and lying on the floor, well away from the action. balancing my single right-eye lens on my nose, feet plugged into my sleeping bag.

The bustling resolved itself into a throng at the entrance over at the far end - a meeting with megaphone for the Turks. The reason for the lights became obvious when two men begin posing in front of them with big puffy mics for a camera - it's Turkiyie TV.

While I was writing Sakir made a rare appearance with a bloke distributing sweets. He said he's been busy packing more stuff in the Truck. He was still annoyed about the possibility of the IHH men taking over our wheels further on, although he thought siamak's plan to keep, he said, exclusive 'ownership' of the van he was driving, wasn't the answer, - but it was pretty much what he, Sakir, wanted to do with the big truck. 'If 'they' don't accept what I have to say, tough. If this doesn't work out, I'll just take the keys.'

He wanted a full meeting of the Bristol "C" team, but we couldn't fix that, to get everyone in one place at one time. A message came next day, **20 December'09** from Mohamed in Bristol - BG Link committee had decided the Big Truck must stay in Gaza, contrary to Sakir's desires.

We were packed and ready to drive out at seven-thirty. The confusion about how to manage our fuel expenses continued, and Sakir mentioned Siamak wanting only to pay for the fuel he used; not contributing to the general pool. I tried not to listen too closely.

We now headed for Kilis on the border, and from there to Aleppo in Syria.

As we drove through the fog-bound suburbs with seven Ks to Kilis, we passed one more waving man. I remember now that as we approached Adana, on a dark, rainy windswept bridge, four men were out, albeit sheltered by the upturned back door of their van, with a poster and flags to welcome us.

And at the Turkish bingo hall banquet all we really wanted was somewhere to rest, do laundry and shower. But we were to be feted as honoured guests.

Going through the border was a doddle although it involved a lot of waiting. On the other side I saw a big welcome poster with the sun-bleached portrait of the President. This is nothing on what was to come. Through the final barrier we had a mosque to our right, and on the left, over a tarmac space big enough for a small game of football, is a stretch of tenting with rows of seating inside, banners welcoming the Palestine Convoy of independent member of Parliament George Gallowi. And tables laid with roses and red carnations which the groups of men and women pressed into our hands, plus glasses of tea or tiny cups of killer coffee. As the border guards, police and army looked on benignly, the little crowd rapidly grew until the whole place was packed. Boys dance in circles. Two great rows of teenagers lined up with flags and presidential lollipops. Mostly from the local tech college, who had got the day off. Our own cameras were shooting wildly, and well matched by the Syrians'- many of us were interviewed. I was asked if George is with the convoy and had to reply, 'Probably not - but he is travelling the same way.'

       We agreed there are two kinds of democracy, 'democracy' and American democracy'. I said 'Respect is hoping to introduce democracy to the UK.' My interviewer concluded by shouting 'I love you!'
I said, 'I love you, too!
We embraced twice, warmly. After speeches, smiling, talking, waving for about ninety minutes we left. The country - open and quiet mostly, but every now and then we passed a group of farm workers come out to wave. The first little town we went through, and all subsequent ones, had rows of schoolchildren waving their hands. After the first town we had a wait of about fortyfive minutes to allow the stragglers to catch up. 'We' are group "C" - and for once I was at the head instead of catching up at the rear. We must have got the Really Big Deal welcome.
There's a little roadside office here surrounded by the dusty yellow farm buildings- the guy behind the desk invites us in - those of us who can crowd into his tiny office, for glasses of sweet tea as we sit., shoes off, on his sofas and little carpet.
Obviously Syria is on high alert. Every school on the route must be ready and willing to provide a 'rent crowd'. It's a good feeling, anyway, and we are happy to keep the children happy by 'veeing' or waving back. The occasional spontaneous group of adults counts for a lot as

well.

Another unscheduled stop was after Tony caught up with one of the vans, C10, which kept overtaking, and yelled abuse at them while we were neck-and-neck. He's a hard man! Everyone got to have a shout and it seemed to be resolved. Then a local family materialised and wanted to tell us we are fab.

It was actually a regrouping to go into Aleppo as a strong bunch. Monica told me she was off for a 'P'. Then we all left, with no sign of her. I tried yelling at the bushes - very thin and scrappy bushes - for 15 minutes (felt like it anyway) then Tony blew his top and said if I want to wait for her, I can bloody walk too. 'Don't get your knickers in a twist,' I shouted, 'You won't help things.'

He got his own back on me when we stopped for diesel and he had dollars and I didn't. Told me I knew he needed money and had no excuse. I had loads of money! Somewhere... We caught up with part of the convoy in Aleppo, which is a fine city with handsome mosques and a good brass band, set up to play for us as we took the road out to Damascus.

Out there, Tony managed to overtake 'C' group and we waved them down - we discovered what we suspected was right - Monica was in another van - '7', which had gone ahead for a toilet, but although she had asked Shakil to tell us, he hadn't.

After those lovers' tiffs, onwards, into the romantic sunset over Damascus! fifty miles out of town we were called upon to halt at the Tower Hotel. Its tourist gimmick is to have a cheese-cut -shaped cage outside containing two red-arsed monkeys which visitors may feed little biscuits. The cage is narrow but high, allowing room for a bit of fake tree which the prisoners to sit on when they get bored scrambling around on the floor. There was no evidence that they might be taken in for warmth. We were all welcomed and given cups of muddy coffee. After a while word went round that there was a 'reception' for us twenty yards along the road in a paling-enclosed terrace. By the time I got in, struggling with a sticky pastry which had been shoved into my hand, the convoy visitors were seated, and one side of the square taken up by apparent dignitories. I caught a speech and a half, then it was over. We were on the road again.

But 200 miles on we had to stop at a very grand hotel which was surrounded by well-wishers and fans. We entered up the steps, a row of public on each side. the interior was hung with drapes to resemble a huge tent, with a huge chandelier made of little leaded red and green lamps. It was the big welcome from the Syrian Red Crescent. 'Homs branch welcomes the convoy of messengers of peace and givings'

Lots more coffee was given us, and lots of flowers. Speeches were made about Palestine, George Gallowi and us, in Arabic and English. Many of us had just made a dash for the toilet first of all. Finally, we left, a Red Crescent guard of honour lining the steps and many photos taken. I and the American lady, who made a speech and got most flowers, were the last to leave, and felt like Hollywood stars. I talked to a Syrian, whose first question was 'What do you think of Syria?' I ended promising to return - if I could - and he invited me to stay on his farm.

Tony hammered on, driving tirelessly until we reached a roadblock. We hoped it wasn't another 'welcome'. It wasn't! I couldn't handle any more enthusiasm. The hotel was beyond our expectations - we were told we would get to stay in a hotel. At first we though it was just a joke, then we (Monica anyway) thought it would be a B&B. It was a gigantic marble palace. En suite rooms. We three sharing. Hot water! A real bog! A shower! A telly! With us on it!

Food of course was in the deal, served in the vast restaurant beyond the swimming pool. The next day, **21 December'09** Monday, was a genuine day off. 2 bunches of us hired taxis into town. We were not on the edge of town; it was the Sahara Tourist Complex. It was a 20 minute journey to town by fast car. Past old village houses, a fantastic growth of vertiginous tenements clinging to the top of a pointy hill overlooking two twin factory towers, half as high as the hill, apparently. Damascus appeared way down in the next valley; we could see a heavy purple-grey layer of smog hanging over it, above which the hills and sky were clear in the winter sun. As we descended into town my eyes started nipping.

The taxis parked, in a main street, we agreed to all meet again at three-thirty to taxi back our various ways. Monica came with me to watch me fail to get several cash machines to take my card, lent me $40 and we got thousands of Syrian Dinars at the cambio. Next: an empty hotel restaurant in lieu of a café for coffee (Monica) and tea (me). We relaxed at our table; through the window was a fine view of the central nineteenth century square with sooty old column and palm trees, but we couldn't resist watching a trashy Syrian pop video on the big screen above our heads. We left, both tempted to return some day for a stay. But now it was on to the internet room. I did half an hour and left Monica to it, wandering off to the old city, meandering through the narrow lanes and passages to the Big Mosque which I thoroughly explored of course. More wandering; the really old houses are part of the fabric of the city though they are fit only for birds and cats. Some top floors have slowly leant farther forward over the years, their wood frames crazily distorted - some so close to their opposites there is barely enough room to insert a fist between. I was reminded occasionally of the dark mysterious closes and basements of my Glasgow childhood.

Overhanging the stream that follows the north wall of the citadel was a filigree balcony, lit obliquely by the late afternoon sun. It was hung. as was the white wall behind it, with hundreds of individually crafted belts and leather waistcoats. A venerable craftsman quietly worked out there, in the setting sun, with a constantly changing flock of slightly exotic local birds feeding at the hanging bowl of bread, or perching on the roof or railings, throwing their shadows against the wall as they took off.

We were expected back at the hotel for a 'reception' at four. On the hour we were ushered to the dining room for an unexpected dinner. The next rumour was that there will be a press conference at <u>seven</u>. At five-fifteen, one of the Irish team. Phil, hurried into the room with the latest news: it's on <u>now</u>. Another conference room attached to the hotel, reached through its maze of stairs and passages, was set up for the TV people to get the hot poop from George Gallowi and others onstage. A large audience was already in. After this there was nothing much to do but hang about. But luckily I left the hotel room after a wash and explored enough to discover the reason we had three guys from Palestine sharing our table.

A hall at the entrance to the complex has an interior roof

covered with strips of Hessian in the form of a huge tent - the centre is an inverted pyramid of fine glass or more probably plastic and tiny lights. Below, an audience of, say, 600 was assembled. I stood at the side for a good view, but many Syrians insisted on making room for me in the seating. Then I was moved again, nearer the stage, taking a seat from a little boy who had to share with his brother. I ended up sitting on the stage, recognised as one of the famous although I wasn't wearing a badge or scarf. The meeting began in earnest. George gave a big speech followed by one from Hamas' 2nd in command. I learned that our two nights in this CB Demille film set had been paid for by Hamas. Many more guys got up to say their bit, occasionally interrupted by a young guy on the floor who sounded like a Muslim flamenco shouter, giving a short declamation of praise, to great applause. All of us on stage were given Hamas baseball caps, key-rings, scarves. As George got on stage we exchanged smiles for a second. The evening finished with five guys singing to a keyboard backing, a plaintive but rousing sound, leading into heavy Arabic beatbox. The place erupted into an orgy of flag waving and dancing. Even the walls seemed to be pulsating. By the time I left I felt mighty strong.

Tuesday **22 December'09** started with something useful and positive - Siamak gave me back my razor. I lent it to him back at the start and hadn't shaved since. I wasn't sure if I wanted a full beard again, and decided to give it a few more days... Siamak had got a taxi into Damascus and found a house where there was loud music and drums. Two groups of travellers had just got back from the hadj. He showed me a beautiful blue stone necklace -

said he had to dance a lot for it.

The sign at the harbour says 'Welcome to the Hashemite kingdom of Jordan'. On each side of the first checkpoint were ten-foot high concrete walls with a fence and earth mound on the Syrian side , extending far away on both sides. Big walls are in the culture here. It maybe wasn't the Zionists' invention. After three hours in the sun, going through several checkpoints, we were still waiting to get into Jordan. We had also had to decant from our vehicles as each one was subjected to a gigantic x-ray on two rails, each side. The total space taken up by the marshalling yards here must approach the size of the Duchy of Luxembourg. The last was surrounded by another high concrete wall.

Earlier, George G had told the crowd that there was another four tons of aid waiting to be loaded onto the convoy by us, before we went to eat. After wandering about, looking for this aid or someone who could tell us where it was or when it was coming, we gave up and ate. In the morning there was still no sign of the four tons. Maybe George meant four boxes, we wondered. How big was a ton? But 'tons' sounded better for a speech. Anyway, there was hardly any room for more stuff in the vans as it was.

Monica, the indomitable girl guide, boiled water for coffee in our room. We all had something to nibble at, and at four we were given our passports back and allowed forward a little. Another delay; no one could say why. A girl came round eventually telling us all to claim that we don't have our passport, and not to hand it over if asked. This was utterly baffling of course. At last, as the now dark area got cold and some friendly border guards handed out some apples, we discovered that the authorities wanted us all to give them our passports as a guarantee we wouldn't try to sell our very publicly funded vehicles, stuffed with aid and covered with Palestine/Gaza slogans and sponsor IDs. In the end we agreed for the driver of each vehicle to surrender their passport, which we had to trust would be returned at Aqaba.

The journey was held up several times for up to half an hour- by the police parking at our head- then slowed to a crawl of half a mile per hour. We passed police cars parked, hazard lights on, on side roads, put there to block any attempts to escape from the grindingly slow procession. Not that anyone would risk leaving the main road - it could take days for us to find each other again. Locals were caught up in the jam, but many of them were happy to see us and waved or gave us the V sign. As we entered Amman the police presence faded - their final act being to split us into two or three parts with gaps of a quarter mile between, using the lights, their cars and traffic cops in camouflage gear. Following our leaders, we winded into a carpark surrounded by buildings that could be offices; all the city looked as if it was built six months before. After jamming into the park - a bunch of attendants nearly coming to blows over where Tony, Monica and I could park, we decided to get our gear out in case we were staying here. We didn't know if this was a stop for a meeting or for the night. Until we got this far into the city we could have been camping out. Some of us struggled up a ramp to the lights and pavement - the main road. Lucky! There was a young guy there, just to usher us across the road, up stairs into an office or function building - banner over the door welcoming the convoy and signed 'Professionals Associations'

(Professionals Associations Council - a TU organisation, not business.)

There was a huge meeting ongoing. George had been addressing the crowd. But we were ushered to another room where there was lukewarm meat pie and yoghurt served. Hotels had been organised for us: separate for women, men and couples - rooms for three - we were to travel in buses head on. Monica was away fast so Tony and I teamed up with another guy. But at our hotel it was just two to a room. The bus was just wide enough for seats at each side and heavy brown curtains covered the windows, although we could open them a little and peek out. It was obviously an expensive hotel. A double bed each, furniture made of real wood, dreadfully overheated.

On Wednesday **23 December'09** I had a Lie-in; woke with mild headache due to the overheated roomalthough the bed was nothing but perfect. I had a shower and a good shit. Life can be good.

Then down early for breakfast - giving two girls the big smile. Got blank stares in return. Two men got up to leave from the corner table, one being George - I recognised the back of his head. I tried walking into town to find (A) an old bit and (B) a bank that would accept my card. But it's just one big motorway system. There are sparsely spaced bridges for people, but the only way to cross the road is to take your chance with the traffic. There were two nearby crossings but as with much of mainland Europe, all drivers ignored them entirely. Perhaps the 'common law' is that it's only illegal to knock you down if you're actually on a crossing. It's a

dry, dusty mile to the corner, a mile to the next, a mile to some little shops where I grabbed a fruit drink and a notebook. All under the merciless blast of the sun. I gave up my wandering - we were out in urban suburbia and it was no fun at all. Major routes for cars, side streets full of high-class apartments, everything apparently built six months ago. Or the old bits, maybe 1975. On my return to the Jerusalem Hotel I found and used the internet room. Why not? En route I tried the Bank of Jordan's hole-in-the-wall. "Transaction denied for this reason…"
If I wanted to buy any diesel in this country it would have to be by plastic. If the garages accepted my card. At the hotel I shed my shoes and relaxed in my socks in the posh lounge with tea while any press junkies among us got the bus to yet another press conference with George. It was definitive mad dog weather out there, and nothing about this city called me out. I knew there were two museums and a Roman theatre, but to do them would only be a mindless 'ticking-off. A crowd of fellows, who gradually filled the lounge as dinner approaches, obviously felt the same. As soon as I eat, I planned to sleep. 'Fuck the tourist stuff!' A day like this in Istanbul would have been better.
Having looked round the local shopping mall on the way back, I went there again to buy a present after taking the reception man's advice about a working cash-machine (just fifteen minutes down and over the road) and got cold drinks at the nearby garage to take back to the bedroom. BBC TV news and sleep.
      Instead of joining the others on the bus to our park and last night's venue for free and dull food, I talked Tony into having a proper meal (14D) in the hotel.
We had an early start next day - but there was a chance

that we might take half the day struggling against police to escape from the park - according to rumour, prime ministerial orders were to screw up the convoy if possible, which is what they were doing the first night and what they enjoy. Last thing, the hotel manager came to our door. Do we want free pizza? It was organised for the convoy instead of the free meal, I later learn. La, shukran, I said, naked behind the door.

24 December'09

An hour waiting in the car park where our bus delivered us. George's right-hand woman told me that the police had orders from P.M. level to stop us from leaving, but the delay was apparently nothing to do with them. Kevin ran round, telling us all if we did't leave now or in five minutes we would never get out of Amman. We had been poisoning ourselves by keeping motors running and revving - I for one was very keen to get the hell out. But first there was a press conference. The only part of which I could hear is that we should get rid of all Hamas hats and scarves before we get to Egypt. I would end up giving all mine to the eager children hanging round outside the 'camp' gate.

Off on the road to Aqaba,. Looking back, I saw the heavy blanket of smog draped over Aman. Stop outside Al-Karak at a spot with two snack-cafés. There was a long tent and seats set up. we were surrounded by guys thrusting canned drinks and bottled water at us. Some of us bought coffee. A youngster - Suleiman - invited me to his smaller shack for a seriously strong and sweet coffee. He's Palestinian, and refused an entry visa to his own country.

I backtrack to the tent, where I saw rows of Arab gents seated facing the sun and a tiny stage was placed on the incline up to the road. George got up and spoke, inter-alia thanking the King, President and police for making our journey through Jordan so welcome, and hoping that President Mubarak of Egypt will please let us in.

120k north of Aqaba, out in the desert, we stopped for an even bigger celebration. Little bags of water bottle, swiss roll, tinned fruit juice were handed out and George gave in return another speech. As we left, spam rolls were thrust through our windows.

As we descended through Wadi Rum from the plains, the landscape grew harder. We were surrounded by rocky mountains and the occasional mini-mountain jabbed up through the flat sand closer to the road. The ground was lighter, almost salty, and the haze of the setting sun lent everything a softly romantic pastel shade; even the stately grotesques towering on the horizon. When we arrived at a lorry park, the Rumour went round that this was our destination. Getting out was optional though, and I almost stayed where I was. Everyone strolled about, hoping as usual that someone would tell us why we were here and what would come next. I remembered that Tony had left his window open, jogged back to our van to check. I was right It was open. When I returned to the centre of the park it was less busy - There was a bus. As I got close, a gent officiously ushered me aboard. I saw other voyagers already inside so I joined them. One of them as I asked, was able to tell me all he knew: 'there is food, and there are toilets at the other end,' he heard, 'so one of them has to be a good reason for being on this bus. I agreed in principle. We were going into Aqaba. The next stop was the local headquarters of Hamas with mosque attached, Mótah Street. A big sign on the side read DR.BASSAM BAW'NEH OBS & GYN

A huge crowd assembled in the open space behind this office building, very unlike a mosque. I was in time to hear speeches by several guys with interjections from a nutter in the audience who had been given a mic, leading the crowd in quick slogan chants involving Allah. George gets up to say, in short paragraphs, followed each time by his translator, and usually the idiot in the crowd, that the harbourmaster had refused to allow us on to our ferry across the straits of Aqaba, despite our entry over there to Egypt being Okayed by Egypt. George would shortly be going to see about this. He was the only one on-stage with a decent microphone technique; the others bellowed and roared, their lips pressed hard against the mic, producing pure gravelly fuzz-tone. I heard the good news: there was free food being served inside. Much later George returned with Kevin. The news: we may enter Egypt, but only if we beg permission to go through the (Egyptian) Rafah Gate, and hand over all the aid to the Egyptians. Clearly this was untenable. The women were to be bussed to a mosque if they couldn't sleep in their vehicles way back. Kevin berated us for ignoring his injunction to stay - a bus-full escaped from the boring drag of a wait for our return to the park. What bloody injunction? I responded. He must have spoken to a few people who were not inside getting food. We were expecting to return to the car park, and we were bored and frustrated.

I caught Kevin later and pointed out that he can't rely on the word-of-mouth system for spreading hard information. He replied, 'well I'm telling you now, you must stay here. That'll do - from the horse's mouth'.

He may well have meant to reassure me, but all he managed was a serious wind-up.

On Christmas Day I woke up at 4.30 after a night on the softly carpeted mosque prayer room floor with countless others, waves of snoring and wheezing floating over us from all directions as the smell of bodies, feet and farts increased, got back to half-sleep but at 5.30 the lights went on - prayer time. Some guys went back to sleep, but not me! I walked in the dark streets because there was nothing else to do. I returned for a shit, then out again to face the cool, salty, sunny morning wind. Nothing open yet - I'd kill for a coffee - but it was only eight. We had to return to the Hamas fun palace in twelve hours. I found the 'pastry shop', King Hussein Bil Talal Street - and scored a coffee and muffin, seated in the sun by a long blue fountain, accompanied by two predatory but funny crows, perching on the railings, strutting on the marble terrace or fluttering around. I found a small housing scheme in the early stages of being built - just uniform dark concrete boxes, domes, windows, arches, before the rendering, paint and stick-on 'stone-effect' tiles are added. It looked almost as if it had been sculpted out of the ground.

nearby I accidentally found what's claimed to be the world's oldest purpose-built church - c.300AD - mud bricks excavated just below street level in this beautiful garden suburb. Several taxi drivers stop and called for my attention, offering me at a "good price" a tourist tour taking in the castle, aquarium, Eliat, the Saudi border etc. But I had to impress on them that I prefer to walk. Difficult! I bought a postcard - the grey-haired guy who sold it to me, with great effort extracted a stamp from his wallet and stuck it on with much pressing and wetting of his finger. Another, younger guy, the owner of the shop perhaps, explained that the stamp is not enough; I would need three like that. He gave me another card - the two of them for a dinar. I followed him into his shop (of course) and after a lot of looking and bargaining bought one of his handmade coral bracelets.

Some kind soul organised an all-day bus service back to the lorry park to get our personal properties. Tony, Monica, I and others got in a huge car, laid on to fill a temporary bus gap. It broke down in the hills. I spent the last hours of the journey standing in a very crowded bus, looking at the inside roof.

I only wanted drugs, but I didn't get everything; I knew I would have to go back, if we were staying after Saturday. Later, I found the Dweik Hotel - 25D for a cold room and TV that's fucked, view of the wall next door but the roof to swan about on, and it was mine alone! George's latest for us in the compound at the mosque - he was still struggling to get through by enlisting help from among others the Queen of Jordan. I enjoyed the bright noisy downtown streets, just strolling, before a good shower and early bed. I found a tiny cobbled square, on a gentle slope, dominated by a huge central fat old tree and full of geezers cackling over coffee and water pipes - lit in parts by the surrounding café lights. On Boxing Day, I spent two hours wandering town from 7.30 to get coffee - found an 'Algerian café' in a street of cafés parallel to the main drag, and took their proffered 'American style' believing it would be wet instead of short and Turkish. It was Nescafé! A bitter pill; I drank it anyway! The sun was up now and it was getting warm. I checked out the compound - They were serving free breakfast - olives, bread and tea. Later some folk went to the beach but I sunbathed on 'my' roof instead. There was a special muslim fast; George was doing it, but it didn't extend to his cigar. Monica was taking part too. At the compound there was a late announcement event - after a long wait, four to six, a corridor of negotiations opened with the Egyptians. The Israelis condemned the convoy for being 'political'.

After my laze in the sun, I wandered back to town/compound for a rumoured 'song contest'. I was psyched up to do 'Old Shep' and 'Route 66' but it turned out not to be a contest. Whatever, it was part two and part one was the night before, rumour had it. A guitarist and banjo player were seated on-stage. They spent half an hour tuning up and farting about before the banjo launching into 'three jigs' - which turned out to be just one very slow tune. I think he was trying to play a four-string tune on three. The guitarist when he got his shot was so quiet that he was invisible; they were both sitting down. Mohammed from California joined them for a rap. In 'three-four', no less. As he was about to start, George's interpreter interrupted him and they had a quiet conversation while we all watched. The rap was done at last, but the rhythm was very loose three-four. I couldn't be sure that it had happened, as Mohammed was aiming at the floor. Monica and a lady chum stood up to sing two protest songs, loudly but ignored by the clumps of men in suits, travellers and girls in gowns scattered far back. The gathering came alive when the Turks took over for mass musical shouting and dancing. The last I saw of them was when they had to fade out quick to allow one of the many TV crews to do a presentation. Real life doesn't really get a look in! On this trip there was always someone filming or conducting an interview - or being filmed - from the guys with big shoulder-mounted cameras like rocket-launchers down to me with my cigarette-pack camera and chewing-gum-strip recorder. There was also free food handed out here - bready things and bottled water.

While in town earlier, I met up with Iqbal and Husband. We chatted for a while to a bright Swedish lady, and the old gent she was sharing nuts with outside his antique and jewellery shop. Iqbal tried to convince me of Jesus' virgin birth . It was central to her Muslim belief. I suggested some people think it was the priest Zacharius, or a local centurian who done it. Non! She protested, and launched into her litany of puzzling ideas - e.g. Mohamed was the last prophet 'or so he said' - I interrupted, and escaped. The clerk in the hotel also got polemical with me as I passed his desk on my way to my room, and wanted to convince me that God is here now everywhere , and not in doubt, when I said I'd like to wait and see if he exists.

27 December'09 I strolled down to the beach, found ancient Roman remains, one and a half columns sticking up out of the sand, of which they themselves appeared to be part.. A guy asked me over to the street map stand, wondering if I could find an address for him. He got to know my marriage status so he was able to suggest lots of fun to be had in the town for'free' men like me, including massage and Phillipine girls. He could show me of course. Where am I staying? I told him why I was here. He's Palestinian - Abdullah - yet another refused entry into his own country. We parted good friends although I didn't give him any custom. I looked for a coffee café, and again met my new Swedish friend, Ann, sitting in the sun; she asked me to join her for a drink.' I was going to ask you,' I said.

.'No- I asked first.'

We found a place next to the 'Algerian'. I hadn't noticed

it before. It caught a little of the afternoon sun. She talked of baby shoes, of collecting them, they're so cute. Of the time she saw lots in a shop stall and they made her tearful. Others began crying, too - but then she suddenly started laughing, and the whole street began falling about.

She also talked about the '*indigo children*' - who are completely new and have no previous life. And her husband. I admired her tiny reading glasses, which she immediately insisted on giving to me. She was going home that day, eleven-thirty, and wanted to say goodbye to all her new friends first. We were both at the Zweik, so I rushed to my room for a copy of my 'book' for her. After a quick check at the compound to see if there was any hard news (no) - I returned to see her off on her bus. Then the manager, who was 'on-side', cooking that night's mass meal for five hundred along the road, told me that as I'm Viva Palestina I get a new and better room. More my stuff. I wandered back along the dry and dusty sea-view road to the compound/mosque, chatted to Ralph from NY about the convoy, cops etc. Lay down in my new room with balcony view of the street. Long days - it was only three-twenty! Outside, VP guys were handing out fliers for a meeting with George; and sure enough, when the deep purple fell, all was set at the compound. Rows of seats there had been set up facing the little outdoor stage. It was a big gathering of the Muslim Brotherhood and Hamas - and us - starting with a slo-mo film of soldiers and children being handed AK47s Mullah after mullah got up then and bellowed at length. 99% of VP people left, to meet at a café in the café street. George joined us there having given a wee speech to the unconcerned at the compound. I gave up trying to get the slow-witted people to serve me in the café and joined the crowd with George next door. He had hard news: we were to go <u>back</u> to Syria and sail from there - while the Turkish Consulate was continuing to pressure on our behalf. We all left- Monica to an internet room I found, doing a five-minute email thing. I took her for a walk to the pastry shop - she sneaked into the bushes beyond the elegant fountains for a few seconds while our coffees and very elegantly constructed cakes were being delivered. Then we visited the ancient Roman church. And I, by guesswork, got us back to ground zero via balmy back streets - gardens, railings, palm trees…

28 December'09 Monday

Seven a.m. – I was at the compound for possible (as rumoured) early update and packed up to go. Nothing was happening; I ate breakfast with the Turks. Ten o'clock - Kevin got up onstage to announce that there would be an update in half an hour and a big meeting. At eleven-twenty I gave up, feeling like a spare prick, and schlepped back to my nice big room for a sleep away from the sun, then sunbathed on the roof anyway. Back at the compound yet again, I heard that the meal hotel's owner had prepared was a local dish, boughari, which is a mountain of rice with chopped meat, beans and garlic mixed in and all cooked in a giant pot. I waited for someone to appear to make some kind of statement about what would happen next, but made do with the trusty old Rumour Circuit. Rumour one was that we leave 'tonight'. Rumour two was that we leave 'tomorrow'. I headed to my hotel again, for my clothes, and I tried to find an ATM that 'sees' my card on the way. The one I successfully used hadn't worked since. Did I get that right? Anyway, I was unsuccessful. At the compound lots of people now believed Rumour three which was that we should checkout and assemble here to go to the lorry park for the night to leave first thing in the morning. This one was so popular I had to go along with it . I had a last shower and checked out of the hotel. Three nights, one afternoon: 100D.

At 7.00 we were all sitting around on the pavement(again) outside the compound. 8.20- Kevin was onstage to announce that the bus to take us to the car-park was outside the entrance. A hard fact, at last!

First, Kevin, George and several local blokes were onstage saying what blokes say. George said praise for all the kindness.

29 December'09 I woke at 6.30 - I slept really badly - on the van in front seat. My cold, or hay fever was back. I knocked back some fruit juice while Tony cooked water and I failed to find my tiny bent solid-fuel cooker. I had coffee, a tiny cake, banana, a fig for breakfast, thinking to myself, 'I could have stayed in my hotel and got a taxi here today.'

George appeared. By eight thirty VP folk were sunbathing, drying clothes on the park fence and playing football. So much for the early start... I never like any delay when it's time to hit the road. I was the same back in the 'sixties - missing out on the chance to explore the occasional village or museum or just a café when it meant missing out on the chance of grabbing The Big Lift. Always all-or-nothing. Nine o'clock- we left. Held up in the Wadi at a garage by cops for forty-five minutes - stop for eats at tiny town: one donkey, one garage, deep blue sky, kids playing. I felt morose although there must be worse places to be delayed.

I copped paracetamol and a hand-built lemonade

from Monica, who also had the cold.

We skirted the industrial suburbs of Amman - it takes a lot of skirting. Friendly waves from the pavement and passing cars. Miles from anywhere, outside the office building of the Jordan Post, a great multitude of men, women and children were flag-waving, signing and calling in Arabic and English "Thank you very much." - Thirty packets of biscuits were chucked in through our windows. It was embarrassing - If all vehicles got the same treatment we might be done for biscuit smuggling. Women were joyously chanting anti-Mubarak slogans - or a slogan including a mention of Mubarak.

The sky grew grey and cold as we journeyed north. Two hours to get through passport control, mostly waiting in a dark park for our passports' return. After a one-hour wait in <u>another</u> dark park for no reason except that the Jordan police decided to divert us there.

My cold No. 2 was dreadful - not the worst, but not ideal for a travelling man. Shakil came round, stuck his head into our cab, and did a hilarious, uncanny imitation of a big angry passport policeman. During the trip he had gone through a series of personas, and with his rapidly growing hair and heavy black beard topping the natty camouflage jumpsuit had got to look quite dangerous; the big surprise of the trip was the day shortly before we started coming home when he got a serious haircut and re-surfaced as 'Mr Patel'. After his comedy routine he told us: we're all getting to stay in the Sahara Hotel again. And first a meal has been set up for us at a restaurant. " No no no," we three oldies protested; we only want to sleep. Especially me. Hay-fever had got to me; now phlegm was causing chest pain as I breathed. The stop at a huge glass-fronted, brightly-lit 'fun palace'

and restaurant outside Damascus: there was a double line of grinning welcomers awaiting our hearty handshake. Inside, waiters shot around the tables like pinballs, huge circular trays balanced high on one hand. I was like a child again, wrested from my bed to stand on the table in my pyjamas for the amusement of the grownups. The music was too loud, the light was too bright, and I wasn't even hungry. I had to converse with the native Manhattanite about his skin being saved in some way by the I.H.H. As soon as Tony went out to the van I followed, to get in and lie down. We got to the hotel about twelve-thirty. I was sharing a room with Tony and Monica, and was last into the toilet; I sat down and got comfortable - an epilepsy early-warning started: everything in the bathroom went 'solid' and I got two warning flashes. I got up and out, made a dash for my jacket and drugs but couldn't recognise the jacket pockets. I got undressed, took next morning's tablets, leaving lots of pills on the floor, illogically took off my watch and stuffed it in my pocket, flopped on the bed.
Monica tapping my shoulder…
'Cliff, are you OK?'
'What makes you think I'm not?' I mumbled into the mattress.
'Here's some water, to take with your medication.'
'S'alright, I did it already, with tap-water.
'\You should get into bed.'
'It's too warm. This is OK, really.'
'Alright…'

30 December'09 Wednesday
Monica had picked up all my tabs and pills and put them into boxes.
- not the right ones of course, But I would have been

asleep in my underpants as she performed this act of kindness. I had had a conscious seizure. The day began with a big meeting in restaurant this morning; with hard facts and a marathon pep-talk from Kevin. I cornered him later and congratulated him on the quality of the speech.

So far: Turkey will pay Egypt 5 million ransom and IHH and the Malay Government were paying for most of the boat charter from Tartouse. We would only pay $139 - what we would have paid for the originally planned cruise from Aqaba before the harbour-master received 'instructions' from Egypt to refuse us passage.

Later: as the balance changed, rumour and supposition again took over. We were staying here another night. Probably. Yes. Get our rooms back. I couldn't get money anywhere for my ferry-fare, out here in the sticks. Monica lent me <u>another</u> $20. I asked Sakir if he could, as our leader, lend me $120. Incredibly he said yes without blinking.

Tony, Monica and I, with Dave go into town - the local interesting and slummy main street, to try unsuccessfully (me and Dave) to get money and do internet. I knew I would have to look at getting a different flight home from the one I had booked before embarking but I couldn't contact the flight booking agency to cancel.

Dinner at four-thirty.

I paid the hotel my last 500 Syrian pounds for their phone to London to cancel my flight (2 January) after Monica gave me a telling-off in the bedroom over her gas cooker and coke-can tea - she and Tony had been 'carrying' me for so long and they couldn't carry on indefinitely. I assured her that my priority in Egypt would be getting money. We agreed it seemed to be more 'European' there - and may be more bank-friendly. At Reception the

clerk told me I still owed the hotel 1,400 Syrian pounds for the phone, and he wanted to see it. He didn't even try to understand what a cheque is. 'Where do I spend this?' he asked impassively.
'Your bank.'
'No. Only cash.'
I gave him my absolute last 200 to show willing and wandered off. I met 'Josh', the guy who had a room next to mine on the roof of the hotel in Aqaba and was slightly chummy. I had no room for pride - Really stretching things I asked him as a 'friend' for a loan until we reach Egypt. He squeakily explained that his friend was actually out looking for a money source, and it's best to get it in Syrian, '-maybe he will come back later, or in the morning…'
I went back to the room. Monica was sleeping; as my book was in the van I tried sleeping too for half-an-hour. Tony returned, I decide to get the van key off him, go for my book. On my return, I left the van key plus the plastic card door'lock' which I placed on top of my bag. It slipped off to the floor; I looked for it but it had gone, lost. The others were snoozing but I had to empty my bag entirely to see if the card fell inside. No luck! Monica stirred into wakefulness, to complain about the noise. I said, 'This is absolute madness…' but she shushed me before I could admit to my little disaster for fear of disturbing driver Tony's sleep.
I go out again. I knew the card was stuck down between the wall and the cheap skirting board.
I wandered round the hotel after our evening meal, and found Josh again. 'Any luck?'
'No, I'm still waiting.'
I sat in the deeply upholstered leather Reception armchair

with my book, watching the Reception TV and the passing of midnight. I was alone now. Josh was just too polite to say no outright. It was a long, dark night of the soul. If he had any sense he would have gone into hiding, as I would. Probably did. Why am I here? Why did I cancel the plane? I could just have got it, not got in debt and gone home. I sneaked back into our bedroom, quiet as a burglar. I grumbled silently, 'Why doesn't Tony wake up so I can fix things?'

I got maybe three hours' sleep. I had two problems now. I could fix 'the 'lock' if it weren't for those two sloths.

I gave up waiting. I could see daylight beyond the curtains. I silently fished out the card with sticky tape, torch, bit of card and tin opener.

31 December'09 Thursday

In for the first breakfast sitting: flat bread, olives, cheese, yogurts tomatoes, spammy stuff, croissants, *coffee*. After eating I asked our friendly Quaker if he could lend me cash. He's sorry but he didn't have it. He would if he could. I tried Iqbal - I passed her and her Husband on Wednesday and missed the chance to turn a joke reference into a bit of light begging... She and Husband knew about my phone call; I was able to laugh about it last night, how much it cost and the low value of the Syrian pound. She said, 'Of course. That's what we're for.' -passing me on to a guy beside us, playing the idiot but who had a useful-looking writing-pad. He in turn spoke to Kevin, who would later speak to our group leader Shakil, dealing in emergency payments. My life was saved. I felt better but I would be happy not to see this hotel again.

Tony and I cleared out our stuff. He said he saw Monica disappearing somewhere. Her stuff is gone. He claimed

he can't get our passports unless she was there. I said he got mine before when I wasn't there. He replied, 'Eh?'
I gave him the key and he was away to Reception leaving me to tidy the room. I followed after room check, see Monica seated near the door. She waved our passports at me. As I take mine, we sat down and smiled. Tony stormed over from Reception - 'Why the hell didn't you tell me you were here? I've been struggling to get the passports all this time and you've just been bloody sitting here,' he turned to me -' and you knew all about it!' I'm sick of the two of you!' After I had a quiet talk to Shakil about Tony's complaints, we loaded up and the convoy was away again, ten-thirty. Monica usually talked a lot to keep Tony happy and awake but now she was silent. She felt 'landed' with us two: the 'control freak' and (me) the 'space voyager'.

Petrol/diesel stop - I paid 950 Syrian pounds. I was suddenly rich in Syrian terms - before we left, Californian Mohammed thrust D21,200 at me. He had heard!

1.30 big sign by Islamic Jihad Movement - **May God be with you. Welcome Palestine Convoy 3**
and well-wishers with bottled water on the motorway.

Motorways here, and in much of Europe, are not like the regimented routes in the UK. Farm fields bleed into them and they will accommodate the occasional roadside food stall. Much more friendly. I remember getting busted and fined for walking on the grass, on a slip road leading away from the motorway where I and my friend Sandy had just been dropped by a lift, in Germany, 1966.

We pass Tartous, and another friendly crowd, and more on a bridge over the motorway. Onwards to Lattakia. A dirty beautiful harbour city, red sandstone Roman column poking up through a hole in the slum. We passed through and out past coastal low-rise 'barrio' to a seaside "student camp" resembling a detention centre, which it may have once been. Also a boy scout camp and refugee centre, I'm told. Whatever its original function was may have ended about forty years ago, I guess. The huts were all recently re-roofed but the three cafeterias resembled abandoned petrol stations and the dry lido was full of rubble, the tiled surrounds broken up and their corner posts crumbled and splintered. The high-up street lights lining the grass between the chalet rows and marshalling yard/watchtower lights at the edges of the estate work, as did the fortified main gate with spikes on top; this plus the lettering on the slanting roofed entrance top give the place the look of a detention centre for sure. A lorry got stuck in the mud near the beach; the struggle to free it from the mud, cackling children, sea waves beyond and occasional rocket fireworks soaring and banging behind us were straight out of Fellini.

We were staying here until Saturday. A single ship had been found in Tripoli, to replace the original one lined up, and we minus a few sailing with the vehicles and aid, were to fly there to rejoin.

A giant meal of chicken in wraps, juice, biscuits and fruit salad was conjured up, served in the semi-outdoor canteen. First, we chose which of the abandoned concrete cabins to inhabit. Most had rusty bed frames with foam mattresses and ripped covers. I was sharing with two others who I only knew by their bags left in the hut. All night, occasional fireworks went off in various parts of town, after some mega-politico-religio voice declaiming and soupy music blasted out at distortion level at the bandstand between the entrance and canteen, and the rows of 'chalets' which were lined around what may have

been playing fields but were now huge unkempt areas of long grass.
I had chai with the Turks, Mehmet, Muamar, Simi and others. They got set up for a party round a table outside their hut. I saw they were always going to be well-organised and hospitable. . Where there's a pot of tea, there's a party. Someone got a fire going I added a few bits of wood. Monica got some logs. The Turks broke into song as I recorded my report for the radio. It was a hogmanay to remember. There was a full moon so bright that electricity was hardly needed, with a partial eclipse. Later the night was ineffably beautiful. There was a blue light so strong it was almost palpable. I felt I could reach out and touch the old farmhouse and palm trees next door over the dry-stone wall, and the blue would rub off on my hand. My one room-mate, Dane, joined me at three a.m; he was in a van that went to town, got covered in bodies like flies on shit, two of them getting inside the cab round midnight. He was terrified but got good video shots. He was one of several guys filming the whole trip. He watched us; we watched back with our little digitals and mobile cams.

On **Friday 2 January'10** I walked round the camp, six-thirty - eight-thirty. I went out to see if ATMs were close. This area was lo-rise, lo-income hi-density so it was a long walk through the crowded market street. It got warm - I decided to turn back, being dressed for the cold night in bed. But I met Monica and joined her in her search for a money changer and shops. We saw the sign for Town Centre and Tourist Town - she said she thought that was where we were staying. Step down from hill. On broad steps into a big slum side street with big tree, just as the muezins broke out, echoing wildly in the air. It was big, wide, sublime. I was struck by the confluence of sensations. I filmed the moment on my tiny camera. A very good walk, and I hadn't used my legs much for a month. I even shared jokes and confidences with Monica. She told me that the Muslim Brothers had dubbed Tony 'Moody Gonzales'. Perhaps one day I'll find out what they dubbed me…We found a café on the way back, neither having found what we were looking for. The café was a club - in English called the Hutteen Sporting Club. They insisted on serving us drinks 'on the house'.

Meanwhile, Back at the ranch:

'Free food - boy Scouty brass band and band with bagpipe for circle dancing by fresh-faced kids in bright outfits.'

I snoozed in the hut, then walked out again, to see the city at night, have one more look for an ATM I could plug into (still being keen to become self-sufficient although the small but insurmountable credit gap had been plugged) and discovered classier bits of the town which looked very like Cromwell Road or Knightsbridge in London.

After the evening free food (packed like the rest by a company called le merideen) I met Shakil. The vans are to leave tomorrow he told me, and we must remove a maximum of 20kgs personal stuff for travelling with.

I had no idea what 20kgs looks like.

We would fly in shifts on Sunday. It was a wild and windy night. I discovered our third mystery room-mate was a girl, who packed off to another hut. I wonder where she slept on Hogmanay…

On Saturday I walked again through the narrow market streets, past the open parkland, up hill and down again to city centre. The road didn't look like getting even slightly more urban. Knightsbridgey though. I run out of time, headed back for Kevin's pep talk then we packed or unpacked the vans and our personal airplane stuff. Go into town for the last time, hoping the 'Tourist Town would have a functioning ATM. It was an advice centre in fact - big exterior with tiny half-built office inside. but inside I met Americans Octavia and her husband, who lived in Damascus and also secked advice. She gave me a donation of 500 Syrians to 'the cause'. It's for me, she said, if I couldn't find an ATM. I would embezzle it for a while, before passing it to the fuel kitty, I told her weeks later. Weaving back through the market I was invited to sit and have a drink by one stall owner. We couldn't communicate except by eyebrow and grunts but did quite well as such. The drink was warm yogurt with cinnamon sprinkled on top.

At the camp, I caught the tail end of the leaving convoy. There were signs that there was a feast; the camp was almost deserted. I lay down in the concrete chalet, on my rusty detainee's bed, in time for a mobile phone call from my lover. I heard her warm, soft voice - she was lying on my warm soft bed at home.

Everyone else came back, by bus They had been at the 'castle'/port, seeing off the giant container ship with a brass band and no speeches. Two new guys joined us in the hut - Adil and Achil.

News: Israel extended its exclusion zone outwards making the boat journey twenty-two/twenty-four hours. We weren't to leave now until Monday night, earliest.

evening Food being distributed at the canteen: a banana and chocolate muffin. I joked, ' I had this for lunch.' and then thoughtlessly wandered along the green to admire the Turks' campfire. They started to beckon me urgently into their chalet , where they pressed a garlicky take-away on me, and fruit juice. I couldn't pretend enthusiasm but I put it away. I realised I should at least learn the Turkish for 'thanks' (Tesekkür ederim) and 'no thanks.'

3 January'10 Sunday Due to the extra bodies in our hut, I woke up three times in a big sweat. It was better after I undid the string I tied the window closed with. Another broken night, ending with some villain thumping on our door (again) at morning prayer time,five-thirty. I walked along to the camp piss-house. one middle-of-the-night I couldn't be bothered with the walk and just sneaked off behind the hut. A bearded person slipped out from behind a bush and stage-whispered, 'it's stardust!'

'Do you think so?' I asked, humouring him. I was half-asleep and determined to stay that way. Someone being mad enough to describe my stream of piss as stardust made perfect sense; but much later I worked out that he had been saying 'There's toilets!'

I preferred the stardust.

After breakfast and a cold rusty shower I decided to take a photo of the brightly coloured camp gate. I wait for someone to walk through it, and get the shot OK. But 'the attendant' sitting in car pointing at the gate shouted, 'Hey monsieur! monsieur! No photo!'

I bowed apologetically, hands spread and back off. I told Francis about this later; he raised his eyebrows and said he was down filming by the sea by the concrete wall when a guy with a gun chased him off.

I took Dane lots of bread and an apple, all of which he stuffed into his mouth. The two others slept almost until lunch, which was: croissant, cheese spreadlets, a muffin.

As he worked on editing Dane picked up a bug and was quite ill. I gave him one of my tummy pills and slouched out to the Arab/ Turkish disco at the bandstand. We heard that we wouldn't now be flying until four p.m. on Monday. On the day I was woken, five-thirty, by the roaring sea.

I next got 'the sick'. I stayed indoors - managed splatter-shit and general wash before the meeting at ten - I was leaving with the four-fifteen batch. So: back to chalet, and sleep. I couldn't eat. It was hot although stormy outside.

The buses took us to the airport. There was half an hour of farting about, shouting and rearranging, standing, standing first. At the airport -sign on plane:
>Departing
>Dear traveller
>prevents the use of mobiles in arena of aviation
>prevents smoking in the arena of aviation

Half an hour into the flight there was a tiny 'oomph!'
We were told we would have to land at Damascus for repairs; the engine was kaput. We had to sleep in the lounge/café/shopping area, dreadfully overheated. Free coffee - and I bought three cream biscuits. I discovered a new trick: I can sleep sitting up.

5 February'10 Tuesday was the day we simply flew to al-Arish, got our passports back after a two-hour wait.

The airport was completely dead - more like a military airbase. (all airline personnel looked military too) We had to pass our luggage through a defunct electronic gate and it was all piled up in a big heap on the other side. We then walked round the gate to pick things out. One of our guys stood on a table with the passports, shouting out our names to give them back out. (Of course, no western union office out here; I was always on the alert for potential money sources.) Red Crescent were set up here, and conjured up free food - two buns, orange juice, water. Five dollar entry visa. 'Tony' Mansour stepped in and paid for mine when they (of course) refused a cheque.

The bus to the port left, five-thirty; two guys were refused their passports back, and three-quarters of us got off to go back and protest. We encamped, parked, in the port. After sundown I took a half-mile walk to confirm we were far way from civilisation… Just as the airport was. No low dives and brothels round this port; only long, narrow roads and palm trees. One lonely corner shop far away.

After a late meal of dry roasted peanuts and water, it was early to bed for me at eight, front seat of our van. I needed it - I didn't want another fit. At three a.m, (**6 February'10** Wednesday) Tony woke me, excited, to tell me I missed the 'riot'. Curious enough to get out and see what he's talking about, I asked around - there were varying versions of what I missed: There were lines of riot police outside the gate, with one 'brother' kept outside. Lines of our people shouting insults. We tore down one of the four gates. Behind the cops were groups of Mubarak's thugs throwing rocks. Water cannon also used. ten of ours were injured, one arrested. What had been clean swept concrete or tarmac was scattered with little rocks and what had been sand was now mud. Guys were standing about, lifting sticks putting them down again. I could see rows of cops still lined up outside ; went back to the van for more sleep.

Riot police lined up outside the gate after our negotiator had left. Demands that only 50% of our convoy was to get through led to a peaceful sit-down demo with chanting - which maybe started off the cops and thugs. Some rocks were thrown back. Water cannons were brought out hitting half our camp. Six Americans who had been out on the town had tried to get through - five succeeded; maybe I had just been lucky to get back in. Rada told me she saw two security men dragged from their car and beaten up by our guys. They were denied treatment for two hours - some wanted to use them as hostages - but the Turkish and Egyptian doctor said 'We don't do hostage, we are doctors.' Rada was pushed away by Kevin who told her' Care for your own people.' when she tried to get the doctor to the injured "cops". Also, earlier, but maybe not early enough, she had been looking for the plastic red roses we got in Syria to stick in the cops' rifles.

Before I went back to sleep I saw one guy being carried away from the gate house. After I, the 'war artist' went back to sleep in my clothes, the cops used rubber bullets apparently.

At breakfast time - convoyers sat around in the morning sun, recriminating and post-morteming. I made coffee in a rubble and solid-fuel cooker. The gate was still blocked by a huge oil tanker. The rumour that we could leave at nine was out of date. I nibbled a handful of peanuts, wished George a hearty good morning. 'I hear there was a party last night. I missed the whole thing.' Half-a-dozen of us had heavy, bloodied bandaging round their heads from the 'party'.

George appeared to have got it sorted - we were going to Gaza immediately except for 59 vehicles which the Turks were delivering to Palestine refugee camps in other countries. Egypt demanded the cut in size, petty to the end. At 4.45 the gate swung open and the very slow progression began. 7.15- our van got through the gate after a long wait at a roadblock outside, the first part of the chopped up convoy hit the road at nine. Our sirens maybe woke a few people. at 11.00 we passed through the Rafah Gate, handing over passports. One Muslim brother joked about my having a 'chequebook'- can he see it? 'Sure, but I only get it out for barmitzvas' - well, OK, it was a silly thing to do, trying to buy an Egyptian visa by cheque, but I had it with me anyway and I had run out of options. Another 'smell-funny' reputation I will have to carry for all time, but it was one-up for him on his mates: he's seen the book!

We got picked up by bus - through the night leaving the Rafah truck-park after midnight to stop at a quite grand-looking hotel, where the one next door, The Commodore, was the one we should have been staying at; but we were too numerous, so a bunch of us found our way to another bus that took us down an alleyway to a much lesser place, al-Zahra - Cold water, double rooms with added foam mattresses on floors for five to a room. Iwas billeted with the IHH Turks, who insisted that I have one of the beds. I tried the toilet - it was as a sit-down but the floor was flooded - a big red-winged cockroach sniffing about the drain. I was ready to brush my teeth and sleep, but somebody got a take-away of spicy chicken meals. We ate. It was real food, the first I had had in a couple of days and maybe the last for one more.

7 January'10 Thursday

I woke early: seven-thirty - Everyone else was still snoring. I was in Gaza with no money, except small change from 2002. We got breakfast served - another spicy chicken wing, rice/flat bread/pickles takeaway -

tepid this time. A bus took us to the 'old aerodrome'. I discovered I couldn't get the money that my sister was sending by Western Union, in Gaza, only Egypt, so I had to accept Sakir's offer of another loan, after he jokingly demanded the return of the first one. I was beyond humiliation.

At the Aerodrome, we watched a Hamas regimental training' - quick marching and shuffling. We removed all personal belongings from vehicles, which were all parked here. Took me just one minute. We stood around in the sun for four hours in total. I felt sorry I hadn't just found out the name of this place right away and asked my interviewee Majed to meet me here. We phoned each other many times. I could only text on this network. It's expensive enough - I guessed - and so was receiving calls.

A rumour wafted by a of big meeting at The Unknown Soldier Square'. Our bus started leaving at five past three and got out at 3.15; I was watching the time greedily as I was keen to get talking to my fellow artists in Gaza- the main reason for my journey. The Square was crowded: convoyers, cops, kids, men in suits. Insanely loud sound system - music and some blahing . But I (with white bag) found Majed (in brown suit) - and we escaped to the quiet for coffee and talk. Joined by his brother Shamikh, co-ordinator of the banned student 'Freedom March' planned for 27th December. I interviewed him. I tried the hookah, but two big hits got me seriously stoned and I had to give up. I had a few little puffs later.

AI also met Hammad, Hanisiam and Tayseer Muhesin of the Palestine Peoples' Party. who, of course, I interviewed.

My friends hailed a taxi, and we, Majed, Shamikh and I

went to a friend's father's house to join a group for a meal. It began with two thirty-inch wide plates of startlingly bright and creepy red crabs, which we tore into. I felt quite well-fed but Majed explained this was only before the real meal. We all trooped into the next room: four giant fish, heaps of bread, bowls of dips cold and cooked and spicy with Coke to wash it down. I was really well-stuffed and treated like royalty! I couldn't manage the last giant fish although I knew it would only be polite - and I was well aware of the dangerous life Gaza fishermen live, being shot at by the Israeli Navy even when on dry land. afterwards, atime for a long talk with all including Bassam as-Salhi - PPP leader, then it was time to jump in another taxi, to the Badra home, where I met Badra senior and we talked till midnight while two Israeli rockets – or bombs- fell maybe a few gardens away around ten thirty p.m. - and watched the telly. with Majed and Mohammed. I stayed the night. I learned that our host for the big meal spent ten years in Israeli jails. He's a laid-back and happy-looking man. His family has suffered more than most- one cousin killed in '52 and another cousin later. One friend in jail for a year.

8 January'10 Friday began with a cold shower for me. Majed got up and 'ordered' us breakfast from downstairs via home intercom. He suggested I rebook my flight on his PC, which I did gratefully. We taxied to my little hotel, later than I would have preferred. I couldn't change the $100 Sakir lent me - it was Friday and everything was closed. The VP guys had left the hotel, with my luggage. 'They've gone to the mosque,' said the desk clerk. I was confused and tried to text the only contact I have - Sakir - But the hotelier was way ahead of me - he phoned for a taxi to take me to Rafah. I thought I might retrieve my

stuff from Rafah and return, so it was no big farewell. Majed asked me to text him when I got to Rafah. We only wheeled round the corner to The Commodore- where a bus was about to leave. I texted Majed a big 'thank you' as we shot out of Gaza on the coast road. There was a long, long wait at the Palestine side of the gate; I found my bags and coat in two hours. Water and passports were distributed and food was passed around on the bus, which stopped dead at Egyptian side of the gate. Everyone got out to avoid cooking in the sun.

two o'clock - after exhaustive security check and buying more entry visas ($15) on the Egytian side of the gate, we travelled through the darkening night and fog. Stopping at a 'café' in the sticks - so we could stock up on sweets and fizzy drinks. We arrived at Cairo Airport, ten past midnight.

9 January'10 Saturday

I noted: 'No one had tickets or could get them unless we paid high sums for flights via Greece, Istanbul etc. Half a dozen of us were herded to an Egyptair desk by a minder. I interrupted my friends' enquiring by insisting on going back round the corner to the Gents'. The man-in-charge said, 'One minute, please.'

'Yes, one minute.' I replied, and carried on.

As I come out there was another 'goon' who had been employed to tell me to go left. No, I say, it's this way. He started looking stroppy but I continued back to the flight desk. I insisted on going to a different window. My 'booked and paid for' flight was neither registered nor recognised. We spent all night trotting from one area of the airport to another, towing luggage and going through security gates, each time having something else confiscated - but they missed my second cigarette lighter.

Several times I had to explain why I am carrying drugs. It's tiresome, opening my dispenser and miming 'brain', heart' and swallowing. They probably just let me through because I look mad.

At eight a.m. I noted 'we are still being shifted around - my special problem being money again, but I had enough for small items. As I now had change I could give Mansour back his loan. No Western Union here though- how to pay for a flight? We have been searched so many times and handed over our passports, I forget how many. Food? A memory. I was lucky I had the feast so long back.' Monica wangled a special deal as she was visiting her husband, resident here. Via another country and back in again.

We ended in a basement area stinking with open toilets. Tried moving a few steps out to the corridor away from the stink, but our way was blocked by a foolishly grinning minder, who said, 'No move. No leave.'

Maybe being a 'jailer' didn't come naturally to him; but neither did being prisoners come easily to us; but by some kind of diplomatic alchemy, one of the IHH persuaded the goons to let him go out of our restricted terminal to get us all $5 sandwiches.

A miracle! One of ours, Arif, got his son, by laptop internet to book him a flight via Australia. He asked us if we wanted him to buy us seats too and we could pay him. He agreed to take my cheque. I had to join the gaggle at the little desk and struggle and beg to get my passport back (for a second) to note my number, from the officer-in-charge. I was not allowed to keep it as I was a deportee. I felt insulted.

I went on the list. Arif apologised - his son got us

on the wrong connection - or ours had left - so we joined another guy's list, and told our avuncular and troubled overseeing officer - who organised a bus to another part of the airport. As we got off, He apologised for our inconveniences and hoped that we don't hold him to blame. I think it was a coded way of disassociating himself from the Mubarak regime.

One forty-five: we assembled and started to try buying the tickets and get our passports back. Like everything else here it involved standing in a room full of incoherent shouting for two hours od more. At three, for some reason, the deal was off!

Now we were up in a clean broad corridor, window view of the carpark, no bad smells. There was even a civilised toilet in a conference room. I gave California Mohammed $10 sandwich money.

I decided to tell the desk man I was being held prisoner , and a deportee and was not allowed out to the bank and did not have enough money for the plane. What should I do? I wanted to upgrade my legal status and get properly charged but instead he got a 'uniform' to shadow me as I was permitted to go to the open area to an ATM for 1,800 Egyptian pounds (maximum permitted) and change it to real money apparently. At this rate it would take a while to get the price of a flight. Arif got another deal set up, by mobile phone to his boy: Al Italia five-twenty on the 10th - Heathrow via Rome 154710256902 RF MSDM7R

I sneaked down the passage to the open area/ATMs/shops, for coffee and chocolate without my 'jailer-cum-shadow, then improvised a bed on the floor. Convoyer Elie appeared. She and another girl had been nagging the F.O. all day, using Thomas Cook's phone, which they cleverly blagged. She hoped to get us free hotels and free flights. She noticed that when she and pals were told they could go and buy Olympic Airways tickets, there was no permitted way for us out and the only option was Egyptair. She realised we were virtual prisoners. I knew that, too. Throughout the day I kept seeing people who appeared to be leaving. Most of them would reappear from another direction. It was like an endless 'Sartre' hell.

There were less of us now, though.

10 January'10 Sunday Ten past midnight: We, the little Arif bunch, were told to follow a goon to get our tickets printed. Instead of just giving us our passports the head guard made a big struggle to find them, sign for them on a list and passed us to a lesser guard, to go to 'passport control' through back walkway to speedwalkway to

Passport Control dept
Chief Duty Officer
next door to
Criminal Investigation
Chief Duty Officer

There was a mall queue at Alitalia but no-one manning it. My four fellow travellers lay down on benches to sleep and were all out in half an hour - but I was under-dressed for sleeping - aT-shirt and sleeveless denim. I stayed awake, angry. Twice I asked about our tickets, then passports - pointed towards the growing queue at the now open alitalia office. At last we were escorted to jump the queue. Told we were too early and to come back at three p.m. No printouts, which is what we were told to come for. Back to 'bed'.

At seven I woke, I had coffee and cereal in airport café (the cereal - puffballs - was a mistake); Later I got dinner, which was more like real food -: a DIY salad, and bought water-pipe baccy to use up the change. There was nothing else for sale…

At one we began assembling to go to exit/ticket issue office. Half an hour watching ourpassports being shuffled - they were still not given back - and posing for group photos. Back to passport control by a tortuously different route and by bus to back door. As we stepped from the bus to the door we felt the Egyptian sun for a brief moment. The first and probably last time. The toilets were filthy - a contrast to the shiny clean surfaces of the shopping areas. We were belligerently standing near passport control office. One officer found another officer, who found with great difficulty our passports, which were assembled with our tickets and eventually handed back to us by a junior officer while we shook hands with the senior officer, who ushered us to the head of the queue (a little horse trading took place)

We sped away. Partially free, with only one more electronic gate to negotiate. When we changed planes at Rome I was asked why I'm going to London.
'I live there.'

This seemed to be acceptable.

Ship ahoy! **The Gaza Flotilla**

After my first attempt to see Gaza and communicate with its artists was cut short by Mubarak's regime over the border, I was determined to try again. The next major convoy was by sea and organised by the Turkish international aid agency, I.H.H. For me it started one-thirty a.m. on Thursday **20th May'10**, when 'two Bristol convoy veterans', Sakir and Cliff, were waiting for taxis to take them to the Heathrow bus. After the ever growing business of near strip-searching at the airport we flew out. We teamed up again with Peter (all the way from the Isle of Wight) and got into Istanbul at 3.00pm local time, Sakir found a hotel near the offices of I.H.H. which couldn't have been handier. Right away we went for a big meal at a local kebab restaurant - I almost forgot how much bread the Turks expect you to eat. Every time I looked like having finished my 4" round they whacked another on my plate.

And Sakir had got us pudding! Made of miniature flakey pastry floating in heavy syrup and stuffed with melted cheese. I did my best... but years later just the memory is enough to bring on that hefty feeling.

We ended the night watching TV installed as an extra on top of our wardrobe. Excellent sound, though all pictures were green.

Friday 21st May - breakfast on the hotel roof, with a distant view of Haghia Sophia.

Peter and I on visiting IHH discovered an interesting new thing- neither of us although we both had our applications accepted online - had been 'accepted'. I, the daft optimist - was sure that this would only be a slight hitch. We met more fellow convoyers including Alex, the star of my 'Cairo Hotel' youtube video.

I'm keen to get out walking but Sakir insisted we get the dedicated bus to the old city. We got into the Blue Mosque as bona fide Muslims. It had taken me forty years to get this far! The last time I walked here was as a hippy in 1968, and I was waved away from the entrance by a guy who couldn't believe I had washed my feet. Of course we did the whole schtick. The endless sermon - all my life I believed that only Christians had to suffer these -, the beautiful musical koran stuff and the Proper Praying. Outside there was a long and deep queue of tourists waiting at the visitors' door, probably taking as long to get in as we spent praying. I was surprised to find that the interior of the famous Blue Mosque is not at all awe-inspiring as I expected from casual descriptions, the postcard and the long anticipation: The huge wagon-wheel chandeliers hanging on chains to within ten feet of the floor effectively lowered the ceiling, and that, and the wall-to-wall deep pile carpeting give it the ambience of a comfortable hotel lounge. I finished with a tour of my old haunts as the other drifted off for a taxi. My own taxi when I get one was an old-fashioned rip-off: It was a journey I could have walked if I had a map, in thirty or forty minutes, about the length of the taxi ride. He probably had the meter running before I jumped in - and I mistook the meter for a radio and the price for a radio station, but I enjoyed the ride.

Saturday **22nd**

This morning we had breakfast inside as it was raining. On Friday we could enjoy the sunny roof. I heard from the Spanish cameraman whose lady friend interviewed me on our arrival that there was a 'press conference' at eleven. Sakir, Peter and I strolled round to the IHH offices after swopping our hotel for a better one. Later a crowd of us piled into a minibus to one of the docks. One of the big ships - Mavi Marmara the (ageing) Luxury Cruiser - was docked - lots of Turks were assembling - flag waving and dancing. The ship was draped in tenement-sized banners. Little pleasure boats and ferries circling about with flags and banners and gave off occasional coloured smoke. Then came The Speeches. Even if they had been in English I would soon have tired of them - increasingly bombastic and even histrionic. I left the thickly crowded close-up for farther away to watch and wait. Finally she pulled out and away, with fireworks in the sky and red green and black balloons clouding up from the stern. We all headed back towards our hotels. These people - so motivated and united in purpose - couldn't just stride home. They dithered - farted about - wondering about taxis (taksis) or buses or the metro. We stopped for grilled fish and a few of us shared a taxi for what I now know is only a half-hour walk. I met my fellow-Glaswegian on this trip, Hassan Kitani, when he used our hotel room with its studio-quality sound (heavy curtains) to edit his film of the Big Send-off.

In the evening Peter and I were again confronted by our tardy acceptances. A bloke appeared after we waited upstairs drinking lots of tea - you are not allowed to sit here and not at least drink tea if you are not shaking hands or eating - the bloke being Durmus Aydin -, who brought us the message. We were not being taken on the voyage as the total number of volunteers had been sent off to the naval security people and it was set in stone. He offered to take my books for Majed Badra and fellow-artists, and Peter's books for the university. Later I discovered that Mr Aydin is not a mere messenger. There is no real hierarchy in I.H.H.- He's the Vice-Chairman.

For a while, it looked like that was IT…

Yesterday was balmy and hot in the dappled Istanbul sun as I drank and ate for what I thought was the last time in a while with my friends. Peter had opted to take a chance on turning up at the dock to see if he could get a last-minute dispensation, but I was sure it was a waste of time. I was quite tempted by the thought of just doing Istanbul for a week. But in the evening after a big meeting at IHH's headquarters and a big kebab at the best local- and prayers in the Fatih Mosque containing the bones of the local warrior hero, known as Saladin (not the

Saladin), having booked into my hotel for another few days and gone along to wave goodbye to the bus, I hung around, filmed an interrview with Sakir and met Belgian artist Julie Jakoszewski, who saw one of the interviews I had been in and was into bonding as a fellow artist. When I told her I wasn't on the list, she said she wasn't sure if she wanted to go. I persuaded her to do it; lovely memories, meet great friends... I should have been persuading myself. I was. She shot a quick film of me and I took her photo in return. Sakir reappeared: 'If I said I had a confirmed seat on the boat, what would you do?'

I was, for once, unable to speak for a moment. I ran back to the hotel to cancel my extra nights, check out and grab my luggage. Back at the bus, surrounded by those about to travel, Sakir gave me a hand getting my stuff in the hold. 'So you're coming then?' He smiled. 'Yes, I'm coming.' I growled.

On the bus down to Antalia, I said, 'You're a clever guy. One of those days you'll have to tell me how you swung this.'

He looked out of the window, 'Oh - it was just one of those things - nothing much...'

In Antalia the men got to sleep in the local sport arena - I never expected to become so closely linked to sport when I was a kid - but the girls all got to sleep in a decent holiday home a short taksi ride away. I bumped into Arish, one of the Turks I palled up with in Latakia; we watched the mobile kitchen arrive and set up for meals where I had been sleeping. I moved my stuff up to the seating riser behind. Then three wise guys, including the Malaysian IHH leader, and a translator. gave us a speech session, with exuberant joined-up shouting from the crowds in the seats. It got quiet enough for sleep after a while. Sleep came easy. But prayer time, four-thirty, started the next day off - **25 May** Sakir hired a car so that we - the Famous Five - us boys plus Laura and Parveen could enjoy the rest of the town and the beach. As Peter and I found, ignorantly giving up a hike within five minutes of the sea it was a long walk to get anywhere, and it was hot. My idea. to go looking for the sea; after my sleep was murdered by the early morning prayers. But before we got as far as the sea we found a shady park cooled by tall trees and big waterfalls; we stayed in there for a few hours I think - no one was counting. After our plunge in the sea and laze on the pebble beach we raided a shiny shopping mall for fruit and nuts to go on the voyage.

One evening as Peter and I were sorting out our bedding in the arena, a visitor, Mahmoud, (came up to us and offered to put us up for the night. It took him a lot of talk, hand waving and eye movement to get through to us but at last we could say 'Oh. Yes, thanks!' - and off we went. In Mahmoud's home he and his wife gave us a slide show of the family Hadj, and we got a good sleep, too.

In the morning, **26 May 10**, his daughter was brought out - she was a real live Betty Boop doll: huge brown eyes that seemed to fill the top of the room every time she rolled them up. We were smitten. Breakfast: we all squatted round a low table with a communal cloth covering our knees as we ate a leisurely big Turkish breakfast - bread, olives, tomatoes, yogurt, cheese, honey, thick prune juice. Well, they - the three of them - were a beautiful family, and I took a good photo of them outside their home. We were deposited back at the stadium in time for another Event - something involving banner-draped tables, flags and speeches, which turned out to be quite passionate. I was handed a Turkish banner to hoist, so I did it, but soon decided to miss the rest although the alternative was braving the furnace outside. I had already completed my paperwork for the sailing as word was going round that sailing time was coming up; very probably this day.

The press conference - if that's what it was - was over by one and we left in our car for the sea at two, stopping for coffee on the way. We walked the last hundred yards to the water and we boys jumped in. After drying out we all put away a great big communal kebab. The current rumour had to be the real deal: hordes of locally-based voyagers began arriving, luggage and farewell relatives and all. A pop-up kitchen appeared in a shady spot by the arena entrance, to feed the multitude.

There was one more hitch for Peter and me at the cruise terminal gate. They had trouble finding papers with our names on them… Later, I took the long walk to the terminal building. The search was as extreme as it is for air travellers; I didn't know yet why. After passing through the scanner gate I had my pockets emptied and all luggage went on the roller, The attendant asked me to open my case. 'My suitcase?' I sighed; I had taken a bit of care over the packing. I pushed it over and unzipped it,threw it open. He waved at it as if to ask me to pull out the contents. I grabbed my coat, sleeping bag, cup, plate, chucking them in the air; and reached for my medicine bag and solar charger, about to begin explaining what they were. He said, 'Enough! enough! no, thank you, sorry.' I kept a straight face, but my body language must have been unequivocal., so when the next guy who wanted to see my passport, explained to his colleague that I was 'English,' I shut up. We were among the first on board and would have the ship to ourselves until nine. We cast off from the docks at Antalia on a blindingly hot Thursday morning, the **27th May**. We were gradually joined on the high seas by the other five ships. The daily routine became obvious first morning, with a 'ping! pang! pong! announcing the first muezzin roar over the speakers. We stopped moving on the 29th. Just after four-thirty PM with no warning we were moving again. Mavi Marmara the vanguard with the others arranged behind in a line. An Israeli spy drone appeared to our stern on the starboard - a tiny pale triangle high in the sky. I tried showering: we were getting short of water so the showers now consisted of a hose connected to a tank of brown lumpy stuff - but I used it and it was a palpable improvement. When I told Kevin, he said he'll wait until he gets to a hotel. He was up for quite a wait.

  I swapped my shorts for my combats in readiness for the next day - we had been told to be ready by seven. Ready - for what? I changed my Turkish Liras in my wallet for dollars from the hideaway in my suitcase where I'd shoved my money belt, which was more trouble than it was worth. Peter, after being interviewed for Channel 4 by Hassan, got stopped by a girl who wanted to know if he was with the German contingent. Like many, she was taken in by his blond hair and military face furniture. Although he wasn't German, she still wanted the interview. He had been a star since Istanbul and a favourite for everyone's film reports; His appearance and 'cut-glass' vocal timbre perhaps lending a touch of class. His habit of throwing in esoteric phrases at high speed (like for instance 'gang agley') didn't matter; it was style! He also, out of mild curiosity, decided to take instruction in the Koran - this doubtless added to his appeal. The convoy slowed to a halt on the 28th, but life on-board continued as usual. Lazing in the sun, strolling round the decks... Every time I met again one of the brothers while strolling, the routine was to greet each other like long-lost friends. I confided in the Malay IHH leader – we didn't bothered introducing ourselves - that I felt a little uneasy about enjoying myself so much. 'But this is the ship of dignity,' he said. Sakir had a shot at fishing off the middle deck; he had a sandwich-sized success. I never found out if it got cooked - but I captured the whole adventure on film. The other small ship arrived, and carried out a triumphal circuit of our ship; the Greek ship came up close too. I got interviewed by Lara for Cultures of Resistance. She said the other boats were full of leftie activists; 'we are all jihadists here.'

'Not all,' I replied, as an old hippy.

'You got on the wrong boat...'

At the time I felt she had a point, but I couldn't go that far now - Mavi Marmara will always be the mothership.

I caught most of a rousing speech from Bulent where he cheered up everyone – and we did cheer - by insisting we could easily repel boarders, should it come to that - and with the distant spy-plane it looked as if it would indeed, although the atmosphere up on the purple-evening top deck, where parties would have been thrown when the ship was a full-time pleasure-cruiser, was relaxed, with some singing. While I got comfortable on my sleeping-bag laid out on the upholstered seating, the rasp and sparks of oxy-acetylene lit up the port-holes to the front deck as bits of handrail were removed for weapons in case the attack came. Then: sleep...

As ever, the prayers next day started at four a.m., but I was relieved to hear only heralded by the three-note jingle - without the usual distortion-level roar of the muezzin. We were at the same time called to put on our life-jackets, which we had to practise earlier at one. The jackets, big, bulky and orange, might have done for playing American football. The 'call' proceeded anyway. I climbed up to the middle deck, overlooking the bow, to watch the watchers, looking at the sea, the black sky, our fellow ships' lights. I tried filming but it was mostly too dark. Someone on the deck above threw light on the men below and out to sea. A helicopter approached, heard rather than seen. When it got close, from where I stood it looked to be almost perched on our top. I saw its propellors fanning above. Its noise drowned everything else. Boats of soldiers were running parallel to us. The 'copter spun away.

Bangs. Helicopter returned. Clouds of dust or tear gas coming down from the helicopter. Loud explosions - sound bombs? Some brightly lit damage was going on at the port side of the ship - I leant out, slicking my arm out as far as possible to get film.

Snappy bangs.

Ratatat ratatat.

They're aiming at the guy with the handheld searchlight.

I'm behind him to get a good picture. I want a good one of the guy with machine gun. Someone slaps me on the arm. I look. No-one there! It was a bullet. Just skimmed off me, though. It stings. Impossible to see if there's damage with this bulky lifejacket. I retreat down inside. If I got hit I would really bleed - with the stuff I use; I'd be no use here. Two ad hoc treatment centres, drip feeds too, have been set up to deal with the wounded. Alex down on the middle landing tells me I have no visible damage. No possibility of going back up just now as all traffic is furiously coming down - escapees and people carrying the injured. Much blood on the stairs. I get out my padded coat for the first-aiders to use as extra bedding, and keep out of the way, in the lounge with my medicine bag. Laura appears, looking for cushions for the 'hospital'. She has just watched one of the injured volunteers die. Through the lounge windows I can see soldiers on the bow deck after red-gold sunrise. A male voice announces: 'The main engine of the ship has been disabled. Please return to your seats.'

A female voice: 'We are civilians. Please stop shooting. We are in urgent need of medical help. We have severely wounded people on board.'

Everyone now (six-thirty local time) sitting around drinking water. The windows were open, which made sitting there a little more bearable. (Despite the constant roar of the air-conditioning it was usually stuffy) I was wrong about the army. Much later I discovered that although from where I stood it looked as if all invaders were coming up from the boats, they were mostly being dropped from the helicopter. They had taken over the deck and upper deck levels and would handcuff anyone going up. A couple of my near neighbours threw their mobile phones out to the sea and one took out a memory card, twisting it to destroy it. Keeping what I had shot was more important to me than hiding it from the Israelis;

I removed and hid the precious memory card from my camera one, containing the 'holiday snaps', Istanbul street scenes I planned to use for a group of paintings, plus interviews, leaving harbour and our sister ships as movies. I stashed camera two with all the attack footage way at the back of my suitcase.

The boy soldiers entered and ordered us to leave, single file, through the port side door to bow. They were dressed to look as threatening as possible: despite the heat inside and out, they were in full battle gear, helmets; balaclavas covering the lower part of their faces and black fingerless gloves. I got out, was grabbed and searched. The first boy told me I couldn't have my little bag of drugs with me. I explained it was my medicine. Sakir, behind me, raised his hand and reinforced my claim. By chance, they let it through. My hands tied behind my back with plastic handcuffs. All my pockets emptied by the two rapid searchers, practically ripped open. My sleeveless Levi jacket left hanging behind me from my wrists and I was holding my bag behind as the search continued. My camera was removed. Also my digital recorder, which the invaders were especially happy to steal. 'Recorder!' one of them shouted. My wallet pulled out of my back pocket, brutally examined and stuffed back in my front pocket. A final, more thorough searcher found a microscopically tiny bulge in my left hip pocket, dug into it and pulled out the plastic wallet with my business cards. They were all chucked onto the muddy deck. At the back he struck gold, crowed 'Memory card!' - he held the not-so-carefully hidden treasure up, passed it to his mate or just threw it into the sea.

I then have to struggle up the steps to the middle deck. All the men had to kneel down in rows just as the Americans do it in Guantanamo. Tied hands. Stress position. For three hours. In whirred a helicopter. It parked above us for twenty minutes, creating a gale-storm effect, whipping up the sea and almost knocking us over. It was a considerable effort to remain upright; anything that was not fixed down was blown off the deck, the life-boats were almost taking flight and the huge banners which had decorated the sides for our leaving, now tied up above us, were getting ripped. The second time the helicopter returned, I lost my grip on my precious bag of tricks, but it was blown against the next guy. By rolling on my side and 'Houdini-ing' my left hand round to one side I could get hold again - but one large bag of pills (from the Co-op) fell out. I had to then keep up the struggle while clenching the fallen bag between my knees.

The 'copter visits were two or three times to pick up injured voyagers, who were stretchered up the gangway to the top deck, but it remained for the usual twenty minutes to knock us about, each time.

My left hand had come out of its cuff, so I was able to wave to a nearby boy soldier, who beckoned me over. The reason for my wave was that I needed to go for a piss. I smiled about the cuff, 'Well, nothing's perfect.' - but he just grimly recuffed me, and replied, 'Not now.' when I made my request. Half an hour later I asked another boy, who vaguely indicated that I may move my arse a few feet on the deck to join the queue. It was getting quite painful by now.

After many more 'copter passes we were ordered to get up and walk round the stern and back, to the port side door back down to the lounge. It was a real mess. All our luggage and loose clothing, books, food had been rearranged in two landfill-type heaps, many cases and bags simply ripped open. As soon as we found seats and a boy gave us a speech saying that we may now use the toilet in a strict rota of one-at-a-time, I beckoned him over and said (with what I hoped was a wry, winning smile), 'I *really* need to use the toilet.' He allowed me to go forward to the door, where my pockets were searched (again) and my hands were freed, but re-cuffed, to the front, on my return. 'Go-go-go!' One of the boy soldiers urged, as I came out. They had mischievously heaped our loose clothing on the flooded toilet floor.

    I managed to negotiate the double-checkpoint system for the toilets twice during our long journey to the Israeli port of Ashdod. On my second return I missed my seat as another guy had taken it. I was pressured by a boy soldier to sit elsewhere; a seat coincidentally in the same corner of the next semi-circle. I didn't see my bag of drugs, and slipped into blind panic mode. So much that one soldier-boy leant over to say 'If you have lost your drugs we will find them.' On the face of it this sounds almost human, although in retrospect I am sure he would have done nothing and only wanted me to sit down.

I noted: 'Nine of my friends have been killed today. I've been tortured and humiliated and face an uncertain future. A guy from Belgium leans towards me (standing is verboten) and hisses -'Hey, hey- look; keep quiet- don't make trouble!'

Wednesday, **9 June '10**

I spent the remainder of the long, slow journey to, as we guessed, Israel, in my original seat, surrounded by Turkish speakers. I should do my homework before I come again. The boy soldiers (at least one was a girl; I guessed by looking above the balaclavas) worked in shifts, changing twice and finally being replaced by others in black uniforms. We got to dock at about eight p.m, and following a long wait very slowly queued to go down to the loading bay through which we had entered a major experience ago. At about eleven p.m. I was stumbling up a gangway to dry land and a walk to a maze of tents containing interrogation desks. Sitting down at the first, just inside the entrance to the big tent, after my cuffs were cut off, I was asked who I was and where I had come from. The boy also demanded to know my reason for doing this. I said I wanted to connect with fellow artists in Gaza. 'Do you realise you have broken the law?'
"What law?'
"Israeli law! There is a blockade.'
"A blockade is not what I would call a law.'
Next, I was passed farther inside to a girl, who while a goon-with-gun looked on, removed everything from my pockets, contemptuously chucked my pen into the dust and put everything else back. A priority was to make sure we had absolutely no recording devices. I couldn't believe they hadn't stolen my money. Yet. Again I had to explain the contents of my medicine bag.
The girl passed me on to the next stage, chirping 'Enjoy.'
Now, a guy asked me why I was travelling to Gaza. I said to meet artists, especially one I had already made contact with, who works on computer.
'Are you an artist?'

'Yes.'
'Do you work on computer?'
'Sometimes, but mostly paint on canvas.'
'Do you speak Arabic?'
'A little, but it's difficult to learn, as they all speak such good English. I know some Yiddish, too. Schlepp, schtupp, schmuck...' - They weren't listening...
They took a particular interest in my passport, gathered round and scrutinising it verry closely. They were amazed that I had been to Gaza before, and wanted to know the precise details of the journey taken to get there; the reason for most of the exotic visa stamps in my book. The next interrogator handed me a form which he asked me to sign. It stated that I had entered Israel illegally, and that I left freely and of my own will. He said that if I signed I would get a plane ticket home immediately, but that if I did not sign, I might be jailed for up to a month. I replied that I would gladly sign if he first put the ticket in my hand. I held out my hand. I had called his bluff. 'You must realise that the longer you stay here, the more you cost the State of Israel?' - 'I am sorry to have caused you such inconvenience,' I replied as I stood to move on.
At the time this meant nothing to me, but later I would realise that with the interest in my passport I was a marked man from then on. I was parked in a chair in front of a tiny camera high up on a stand. On its table there was also a little printer capable of knocking out my likeness four times although my face in the passport-sized photos was really too small for any passport. This, the unsigned paper and my passport were then kept in an A4 plastic dossier bag. Taken to a portable ID machine, a laptop fixed on top of a large black box, I had to press each digit finger on a little glass panel twice.

Finally, the last tent within the tent: A final search. All my money and bank/travel cards removed from my wallet and money belt and carefully laid on a chair. A girl was exclusively employed to rip open all my little boxes of pills in foil and reassemble them, replacing them in my plastic shopping/medicine bag.

Then a really dirty low-life carried out a search more thorough than before, fluttering his hands all over me from top to toe. Not quite thrusting his fingers into any orifices. I could hardly believe that with all this obsessive searching they had repeatedly missed the expensive, shiny little mini microphone in my Levi jacket pocket. Of course it was no longer much use to me without a recorder to plug it into. All my money was carefully laid out on a seat and I was allowed to retrieve it, one more time. Then we were ushered out to a van. Three of us in the tiny front compartment with more in the one behind. As ever with the Israelis, nothing happened for a good while. I had thought that I had seen prime inefficiency in Egypt. Our friends in the back seats called out for the air conditioning to be turned down. We explained that it was only us chickens on board, and that we were locked up too. When the drivers at last got in and we pulled out, the lights went off. I expected the next thing to be carbon monoxide filling our tiny, blacked-out tin box. But after a two-hour journey, (doubtless feeling like twice that for one of my fellow travellers whose bladder was full and whose panicked entreaties to the driver to stop were of course ignored), we stopped at Beer Sheva Jail, way out in the desert.

Two aimiably oafish blokes took charge of our entry. By now it was approaching five am. We were given a little food: bread, peppers, apples, water. And mattress covers, underpants, socks, T-shirts, towels, food trays, toothbrushes, toothpaste. This part of the prison had obviously been a building site a couple of weeks before: a fine layer of cement dust covered every surface. The floor of the hall was painted pale grey to match the cell doors and the chunky railings on the stairs and the balcony leading to the upper rooms. In all the look of the place was like a 'post-modernist' set for Jailhouse Rock. As the cells were opened we grabbed places and with sunrise we got to sleep. I, in cell 2019, was joined by Pakistani TV presenter Serge, whose business card had gone into the mud with my own cards on the boat; Sukir, a gentle and kind professor also from Pakistan, and big, 'all-American' Serbian Stojinjkovic. They all spoke english, as mixed foreigners nearly always do. So my verbal exile was ended. Just in time for bed, as we removed the plastic foam mattresses from their store-bought bags and crashed out.

On the first of June, as soon as I felt up to it I had a shower. The skin where that bullet had grazed me peeled away like dry skin, leaving a purple-red mark which in turn faded away in a few weeks. I had been extremely lucky: although under fire, in the confusion of flashing lights, explosions and gunshots my creative self had taken over and I had been determined only to get a good film clip, a better shot of the man with the machine gun; if I had been standing a couple of inches to the right my wound could have been serious.

We all got acquainted. We didn't all talk to everyone on the boat, but now we got the chance to really pal-up. The noisy and hugely entertaining Ken O'Keefe, renounced US citizen/ now citizen of the world especially Palestine, the East-Londoner who looked like Yusuf Islam's little brother, the Spaniard, the white-haired teacher from Sweden, Dimitiris the Greek.

The promise that we could call home and/or our consuls turned out to be more bullshit. There was a long bank of phones on the wall by the showers but only one functioned, and only with a phonecard. Most of the time our block seemed to be in the charge of 'the Kid', a skinny lad who tried to marshal us into our cells after feeding time, on time but who we defeated by spinning out our long-winded discussions about the meaning of life. This wasn't being run like a conventional jail - only a holding centre until we could be got rid of. Occasionally we were visited by a group of officers from other parts of the jail, including a uniformed woman, glamorous enough to pass as Lebanese, and whom I could only regard with lustful eyes. It could have been a combination of her well-filled skirt, sculpted hair, neatly pressed uniform and my lack of sleep. Some men are put off by powerful women, but not me.

Regardless of the empty promises, late in the afternoon our consuls appeared, the two-man team from the UK consulate in Jerusalem coming round last. (I heard that at one block they had had to conduct their interview with the British inmates by crouching down and shouting through the glass door) I told Roger, second in command, that the first guy I spoke to at Interrogation tried to get me to sign the statement 'admitting' that I had entered Israel illegally and that I was leaving freely and of my own will.
I had seen that one or two who signed got sent to jail

regardless.

In the heat of the day you could dehydrate quickly and it was important to keep drinking. Around ten a.m. I had tried opening a window to let in a breeze; it was exactly like opening an oven door. Roger, who had been making his way round the jail for most of the day while we were lying on our backs trying not to move, politely asked me if I could possibly find him a glass of water. Two of us Brits leapt into action, getting a bottle and washing out a plastic glass. I said, 'You must think we're terrible hosts.'

He said that he would send me a list of legal representatives in a couple of days, in case I needed them, and visit again soon if it looked like a long haul, also taking away my message of reassurance to my concerned sister Jane and pal Ed who had to pose as a relative to get past the red tapirs at the Foreign Office. If he or his colleague made any representations about setting a date for freeing us we were not aware of it, although I was confident that the Israelis wanted us out of the country as soon as possible.

June 2nd, Four a.m.: two guys with boxes of passports wanted to know how many of them matched with us. Only a very few. The lucky winners packed up and left. At seven a.m. a guy entered with a smaller pile of passports. 'The Kid' told us we were going to another centre. I saw fellow-Bristolian Sakir for the first time in a while. We had to wait in a tiny, if high-ceilinged, room for a few long hours, made worse by a couple of us being intent on a smoke, burning up the oxygen. I joined in the objections, and they quickly put out the cigarettes after grabbing one more gasp. Two buses were to take us to Ben Gurion Airport; a one-hour journey. After sitting in the buses for a further hour as they circled about then slowly ground through the exit. We were promised that inside the airport would be our missing luggage.

In a large waiting area, surrounded by rifle-toting guards we had to wait for hours while nothing but lots of paper-shuffling took place at the long 'desk'(three or four tables) before us. Although one of the 'officers' passed round giant rolls containing cheese, tomato, spam, the wait and occasional insulting threats got too much for one of us who angrily pointed his finger at a senior officer- who stepped forward and slapped the pointing hand away. Sparking off a jump-up scrummage - soldier/cops ran in, jumping on top and dragging the pointer or his friend away, flattening him to the floor, handcuffing him and taking him to a room. While other goons sprung forward to threaten us, many of whom were still chewing on our hero sandwiches, with guns.

My turn at last. Israeli public servants/bureaucrats do make the Egyptians I had crossed look like models of efficiency.

I was given the file plastic envelope containing the bad photos taken at the port, a photocopy of my passport and, I think, my actual passport. Directed to a glass-fronted booth where a woman did something below her desk for a while, painstaking and mysterious before handing me back the envelope. A hovering man directed me through a barrier past another boy soldier with rifle. Faced with an airport-style electronic gate and roller-scanner for my nonexistent baggage, I had to go through the usual emptying of pockets. A new one for me: this time I had to take off my shoes. When I had reassembled myself a small blond kid yelped,'Sit!'

Suddenly my calm snapped. I thrust my face forward. 'Do you think I am a little dog, that you can tell me to sit?!'
A besuited lad stepped forward and quietly said, 'You must sit.
'No, I must not sit!'
I sat.
I asked the suited 'usher' that question again, as he politely asked me to move on if I was ready, 'Where is my luggage?'
'In the hall.'
I walked forward. Into the hall. A low-ceilinged room as broad as it was long. Completely empty! Only a desk away at the far side. I could see there was no turning back: right behind me the kid with the rifle.
At the desk a smoothly coiffured guy took my envelope and asked me where my passport was. I said I didn't know - you've got it. The girl beside said 'Now you can go down there', gesturing at the stairs behind leading down to the glass frontage.
'To whaat?'
'To the bus.'
'Wait a minute! I'm here for my luggage.'
Smoothie said it was all sent to Turkey. 'I have to say, I don't believe you. (He shrugged, half-smilingly) And my passport?'
'Sent to the consulate in Turkey.'
I was quite tired, and a little confused. Combined with the smooth man's bland and well-rehearsed (empty) assurances this led to my descending the stairs going out of the door and into the bus - with no passport. I got out again. The boy soldiers at the door leapt forward.
'I must have my passport.'

'Wait on the bus!'
'No, I will wait here.' -I turned to the girl soldier: "Will you get my passport? It really is important.'
"'Yes, I will get it. Later.' - she looked away
"'No! You really must get it now.'(I smiled) 'Look, I'll come with you.'
The two boys jumped at me, shoving me with their rifles and their arms, like angry monkeys. I yelled at the girl as we struggled, 'You stole my passport, you fucking crooks - What are you going to do with it? Commit another crime?'
I couldn't fight back convincingly as my priority has always been to keep hold of my bag of medicine - it's like lugging an extra person around. I had left it on the bus, anyway. Slam! So I was back on board for good.
The filled bus set off for the plane; a crowd already inside gave a huge round of applause as we boarded. Several other crowds joined us, always accompanied by overwhelming cries of victory and love. Our flight was delayed by several hours as Bulent Yildirim, leader of I.H.H., was still being held by the airport/army/police. When he eventually climbed on I gave him a manly punch on the shoulder as a welcome. Not as invasive as it sounds - the first time I came close to him, in Istanbul, he gave my four-pack a really good grope in passing, as a kind of greeting.

Turkish Airlines/the Government kindly put many of us up in hair-raisingly expensive hotels back in Istanbul, a stay which had been planned for about one night, but when Sakir and I, and Peter who had booked our flight together, said we wanted to stay till Sunday they said, Fine. So we were able to combine a little more sightseeing with attendance at two funerals of the brothers who had been killed. And most of that luggage did turn up, in a warehouse administered by IHH. Even some cameras were there, most of them relatively undamaged but all without their media, including the Istanbul street photos I planned to use for a painting collection, shots of cats and kebabs and of course the war footage. I got my passport back - back in the UK - after I had bought an emergency passport and full replacement. The adhesive visas had been carefully unpeeled. On the **4th June** Peter and I did a TV interview in a nearby studio, then we split up for a while; I went shopping for a new camera memory card. The sticky fingerprints of the 'pirates' were still on camera two. I found somewhere to do a large blog, to reassure all at home I was still breathing. Took me a while, using a Turkish keyboard with some keys worn blank. I circled round the lanes of the Fatih district, keeping well into the shade, and emerged into a big anti-Israel march which was heading up slowly towards the city walls.

We had one evening away from the hotel: an Istanbuler who earlier gave us a lift back from the 'stolen property' warehouse invited some of us to his home for a meal, so we got an update on Istanbul driving. Our host and his pal really enjoyed themselves on the freeway, treating it like a giant game. When joining heavy traffic the way is not to ease yourself diagonally out across the lanes, but to drive straight out at a right angle to the traffic flow, then execute a sharp turn in the fast lane. His home was grandly decorated very much in the Turkish manner - in the sitting room, important 'ambassadorial' furniture - big sofas and a TV screen to match. Our hosts spent the evening doing their best to keep me and Peter liberally supplied with fruit, nuts and drink. We did our best to put it away.

When the day came for us to fly home I still had to sprint round the airport, looking for the airport police to rubber-stamp my emergency passport, which none of them had seen before. Sakir and Peter had got upgrades to first class for the flight; I was tempted - but it was only a flight, I thought.

When the entire British contingent arrived at Heathrow, ten p.m. local time Sunday **6th June**, the enormous crowd gathered to welcome us alerted us for the first time to the fact that the attack on our Flotilla was Big News. And from the Zionist point of view, one of the biggest PR disasters in history. At baggage collection, we waited until we were all off and assembled, then made our Grand Entrance. I found myself sharing the lead, carrying our flag with Laura, veteran of all the Palestine convoys; each holding a corner. I couldn't quite decide whether to look 'serious' or 'happy', but as I got close to the cheering crowds I grinned my head off.